ORGANISATION FOR ECONOMIC CO-OPERATION AND DEVELOPMENT

The OECD is a unique forum where the governments of 30 democracies work together to address the economic, social and environmental challenges of globalisation. The OECD is also at the forefront of efforts to understand and to help governments respond to new developments and concerns, such as corporate governance, the information economy and the challenges of an ageing population. The Organisation provides a setting where governments can compare policy experiences, seek answers to common problems, identify good practice and work to co-ordinate domestic and international policies.

The OECD member countries are: Australia, Austria, Belgium, Canada, the Czech Republic, Denmark, Finland, France, Germany, Greece, Hungary, Iceland, Ireland, Italy, Japan, Korea, Luxembourg, Mexico, the Netherlands, New Zealand, Norway, Poland, Portugal, the Slovak Republic, Spain, Sweden, Switzerland, Turkey, the United Kingdom and the United States. The Commission of the European Communities takes part in the work of the OECD.

OECD Publishing disseminates widely the results of the Organisation's statistics gathering and research on economic, social and environmental issues, as well as the conventions, guidelines and standards agreed by its members.

This work is published on the responsibility of the Secretary-General of the OECD. The opinions expressed and arguments employed herein do not necessarily reflect the official views of the Organisation or of the governments of its member countries.

Also available in French under the title:
Florilège d'établissements d'enseignement exemplaires du PEB : 3e Édition

Education plays a pivotal role in the growth and personal development of individuals as well as in the prosperity of countries. The Organisation for Economic Co-operation and Development (OECD) assists governments to develop policies that deliver quality learning programmes and quality learning environments in today's rapidly-evolving knowledge society. Educational facilities are an essential component of the learning environment, and governments have a responsibility to encourage development of innovative settings that inspire and motivate learners of all ages.

The schools and universities showcased in this book are a shining tribute to the commitment at all levels to building quality educational spaces for pupils and communities. This Compendium is also a witness to innovation in design and to successful teamwork: increasingly, governments, architects, facilities managers, teachers, students, parents and communities are working together to identify how facilities can best meet the needs of their users.

Fulfilling the community's needs is only one characteristic of effective learning environments. An international jury selected the 65 institutions presented in this book on the basis of four additional criteria. How is the principle of flexibility

– necessary to accommodate an ever-increasing range of teaching and learning scenarios and technologies – incorporated into the design of the facility? How are environmentally-friendly features and materials used to create a comfortable and sustainable learning environment? How does design ensure the safety and security of its occupants? How can alternative financing mechanisms such as public-private partnerships contribute to good management and planning?

This is the third international Compendium of Exemplary Educational Facilities published by the OECD Programme on Educational Building (PEB). Through its numerous publications and events, PEB informs on how to adapt to emerging technologies, how to obtain maximum educational benefit from investment in facilities, and how to efficiently plan and manage educational infrastructure.

We would like to express our heartfelt thanks to all those who submitted projects for the Compendium. The jury received a panoply of designs, and selecting those for inclusion in this book was no easy task.

We hope that you will enjoy and find inspiration from perusing the exceptional institutions featured in this volume.

Mukund Patel

Head, Schools Capital (Assets) Division,
Department for Education and Skills, United Kingdom
Chair, OECD Programme on Educational Building
Governing Board

Barbara Ischinger

OECD Director for Education

PEB

Compendium of exemplary educational facilities

3rd edition

OECD

The OECD Programme on Educational Building (PEB) wishes to thank the many people who contributed to this publication including the jury, the candidates and the publisher.

Jury

The jury members freely gave of their time to study each of the projects submitted and to agree on those to include in this book. They also offered many ideas which were useful in compiling this Compendium. The members of the jury were:

Mukund Patel, head of the Schools Capital (Assets) Division, Department for Education and Skills, England, United Kingdom; Chair, OECD Programme on Educational Building Governing Board.

Rodolfo Almeida, architect and international consultant representing the International Union of Architects (Work Programme Educational and Cultural Spaces), born in Mexico.

Simone Forster, professor of economics in a High School of Management, scientific collaborator at the IRDP (*Institut de Recherche et de Documentation Pédagogique*), editor of the journal of the *Conférence intercantonale de l'instruction publique de la Suisse romande et du Tessin*, Switzerland.

Mary Molloy, school principal at Ardscoil Mhuire, Co. Galway, Ireland.

Giorgio Ponti, architect and co-ordinator of the Educational Architecture Area, CISEM (Research Institute of the Province of Milan and Italian Provinces Union), Italy.

Candidates

PEB gratefully acknowledges the help it has received in preparing this publication from the institutions and education authorities concerned and from the architects who designed them. PEB also wishes to express its thanks to those who submitted nominations for inclusion but which were not chosen for publication.

Publisher

Pressgroup Holdings Europe, S.A., compiled, edited and printed the *PEB Compendium of Exemplary Educational Facilities: 3rd Edition* for which PEB is immensely thankful.

From left to right: M. Molloy, R. Almeida, S. Forster and G. Ponti

PEB Compendium of Exemplary Educational Facilities: 3ʳᵈ Edition

Criteria

The jury chose the facilities featured in this publication for their fitness for educational purpose and found that each institution demonstrated at least one of the criteria described below. The facilities' construction, design or use was judged to be noteworthy and to contribute to educational quality. Included are newly built or renovated buildings, extensions or grounds. Each project is labeled with the criteria assigned to it by the jury.

Flexibility

Buildings or grounds that are adapted to new forms of learning and research; institutions that make special use of information and communications technology; or special educational facilities. Charactistics include transformable learning spaces, student-centredness, problem-based learning facilities, or provision for students with physical, learning or behavioural difficulties or for "at-risk" students (those whose educational needs arise primarily from socio-economic, cultural or linguistic factors).

Community needs

Institutions that encourage community involvement and/or access by giving multiple stakeholders the opportunity to participate in their design, planning or day-to-day management; by catering to lifelong learning; or by sharing the facilities with students' families or others.

Sustainability

Facilities that demonstrate special consideration for the environment through the efficient use of energy, choice materials, local or natural resources, siting or management.

Safety and security

Facilities that give particular attention to standards, design, construction materials, building management or risk assessment to provide for safety from natural disasters or accidental or deliberate acts of man, for personal and material security, and for the health and comfort of their users.

Alternative financing

Institutions which have used alternative ways of financing capital expenditure (including the use of private financing), or buildings whose life-cycle costs are sustainable.

Readers' guide

Classification of levels of education

The classification of the levels of education is based on the revised International Standard Classification of Education (ISCED-97). ISCED is an instrument for compiling statistics on education internationally. The following levels of education are presented in this publication:

◆ **Pre-primary education (ISCED 0)** is defined as the initial stage of organised instruction, designed primarily to introduce very young children to a school-type environment, that is, to provide a bridge between home and a school-based atmosphere. ISCED level 0 programmes should be centre- or school-based, be designed to meet the educational and developmental needs of children at least three years of age, and have staff that are adequately trained (*i.e.* qualified) to provide an educational programme for the children.

◆ **Primary education (ISCED 1)** usually begins at age five, six or seven and lasts for four to six years (the mode of the OECD countries being six years). Programmes at the primary level generally require no previous formal education, although it is becoming increasingly common for children to have attended a pre-primary programme before entering primary education. The boundary between pre-primary and primary education is typically the beginning of systematic studies characteristic of primary education, *e.g.* reading, writing and mathematics. It is common, however, for children to begin learning basic literacy and numeric skills at the pre-primary level.

◆ *Lower secondary education (ISCED 2)* generally continues the basic programmes of the primary level, although teaching is typically more subject-focused, often employing more specialised teachers who conduct classes in their field of specialisation. Lower secondary education may either be "terminal" (*i.e.* preparing students for entry directly into working life) and/or "preparatory" (*i.e.* preparing students for upper secondary education). This level usually consists of two to six years of schooling (the mode of OECD countries is three years).

◆ *Upper secondary education (ISCED 3)* corresponds to the final stage of secondary education in most OECD countries. Instruction is often more organised along subject-matter lines than at ISCED level 2 and teachers usually need to have a higher level of, or more subject-specific, qualifications than at ISCED 2. The entrance age to this level is typically 15 or 16 years. There are substantial differences in the typical duration of ISCED 3 programmes both across and between countries, typically ranging from two to five years of schooling. ISCED 3 may either be "terminal" (*i.e.* preparing

the students for entry directly into working life) and/or "preparatory" (*i.e.* preparing students for tertiary education). Programmes at level 3 can also be subdivided into three categories based on the degree to which the programme is oriented towards a specific class of occupations or trades and leads to a labour-market relevant qualification: general, pre-vocational or pre-technical, and vocational or technical programmes.

◆ *Tertiary education (ISCED 5/6)* programmes have an educational content more advanced than those offered at other levels. Programmes can be largely theory-based, with a minimum cumulative theoretical duration of three years' full-time equivalent and designed to provide sufficient qualifications for entry into advanced research programmes and professions with high skill requirements, such as medicine, dentistry or architecture; provide practical, technical or occupational skills for direct entry into the labour market, with a minimum duration of two years' full-time equivalent; or lead directly to the award of an advanced research qualification, *e.g.* Ph.D.

Typical starting age of students[*] in the 20 countries represented in the Compendium, by level of education

◆ Pre-primary education   (ISCED 0)
◆ Primary education   (ISCED 1)
◆ Lower secondary education (ISCED 2)
◆ Upper secondary education (ISCED 3)
◆ Tertiary secondary education (ISCED 5/6)

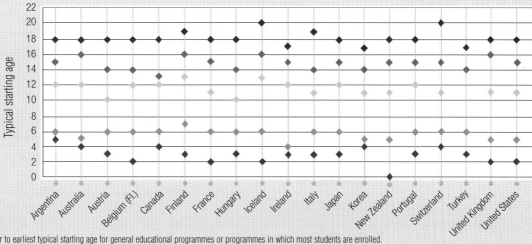

(*)Typical ages refer to earliest typical starting age for general educational programmes or programmes in which most students are enrolled.

Source: For OECD countries, *OECD Handbook for Internationally Comparative Education Statistics: Concepts, Standards, Definitions and Classifications* (2004), OECD; and for Argentina, *Education Trends in Perspective: Analysis of the World Education Indicators* (2005), OECD, UNESCO Institute for Statistics.

Lend Lease

The changes rapidly transforming the ways we live, work and recreate are also changing the ways we need to think about delivery of education services.

In every country people are searching for the most appropriate education service and the best ways of delivering that service to communities, so that everyone will be a learner all their life. The social, economic and environmental sustainability of communities depends increasingly on education and training services that are responsive and accessible to all.

Lend Lease knows that the communities it creates around the world – whether new or existing – must have outstanding education services if they are to be successful and if that success is to endure.

One aspect of getting education service right involves working with partners to provide the right built environment for learning. What constitutes an appropriate place to learn is also changing and the OECD Programme on Educational Building provides a valuable service by again publishing a Compendium of Exemplary Educational Buildings.

We believe the Compendium's main purpose will be to help policy makers identify those trends and characteristics which reflect the changes occurring in education services.

As such, Lend Lease is pleased to be associated with this Compendium.

Ross Taylor
Chief Executive Lend Lease Retail & Lend Lease Communities

Executive summary

Can architecture and equipment contribute to improving the quality of education? Can architecture alone, through its spaces, volumes, colours, exteriors and materials also serve to educate? This third PEB Compendium attempts to reply positively to both these questions and to demonstrate how the design, use and management of buildings and grounds facilitate the learning process for teachers, students and the community.

This latest edition presents newly built or renovated facilities for all levels of education, from pre-school to tertiary, and describes how effectively those facilities serve the needs of their users: students, teaching and administrative staff, and the community at large.

Selection criteria

An international jury, appointed by PEB, studied the pedagogical information, photographs and architectural plans of all the projects submitted. The jury members are listed on page 5.

The jury chose the 65 facilities featured in this publication for their fitness for educational and community purpose, and evaluated and analysed in detail each project using the following criteria (described on page 8): flexibility, community needs, sustainability, safety and security, and alternative financing.

Buildings are not expected to be exemplary from all points of view; a building recommended for its original approach in energy management may not fully comply with the other criteria. However, the fact that one or two of the criteria are clearly expressed in a given project provides a strong character and personality to the resulting architecture.

The jury believes this Compendium presents a new vision of architecture for education, finding that the majority of the institutions are designed and used in a fresh, poetic and inspirational manner. The jury expects that readers, whether architects, educators or decision makers, will be inspired by the examples presented here of innovative and beautiful responses to present and foreseeable changes in education, culture and society as a whole.

All the architectural projects selected, whether new, rehabilitated or refurbished buildings, small rural educational centres or large urban complexes, are creative in their volumes and spaces. They reveal how architecture can not only improve the quality of education but can also foster learning and community participation by reflecting local culture and introducing modern ideas into their design.

Some projects present new solutions to financing, such as public and private partnerships or fund-raising by parents, often with the active involvement of parents and students in the planning and design process.

Projects demonstrating a flexible curriculum and groupings based neither on grade nor age were particularly appreciated by the jury as a major innovation. These institutions offer subtle spaces of different sizes, "retreat" spaces for small groups and "streets" or circulation areas facilitating informal learning and socialisation among the users.

Certain institutions responding to rich and varied educational and architectural requirements provide a variety of spaces, resulting in architecture with great character, well integrated into the urban tissue and allowing community access all day long.

Readers can learn from the Compendium's diverse design solutions, from a giant "happy crate" which houses learning and administrative boxes as well as an outdoor space, to a small urban site whose "outdoor" spaces are located on each floor and on the roof, to the refurbishment of existing schools using contemporary forms and energy saving designs to reinforce educational, cultural and societal values, including safety and security.

Publication structure

The jury wished to distinguish nine institutions which they found to be particularly remarkable; these are presented in Chapter One, which also includes jury comments.

INTRODUCTION

The other chapters are each devoted to a different level of education, with Chapter Two presenting institutions that cover multiple levels. Within each level of education, the institutions are arranged alphabetically. The levels of education are defined on page 8.

Each project is labelled according to criteria, which are also listed on page 8.

At the end of the publication, the reader will find the contact details of all the institutions and architects featured, as well as an index of the institutions by criteria.

This Compendium follows a first edition entitled *Schools for Today and Tomorrow* (1996) and a second entitled *Designs for Learning: 55 Exemplary Educational Facilities* (2001).

PEB

The Programme on Educational Building, which operates within the Organisation for Economic Co-operation and Development, promotes the exchange and analysis of policy, research and experience in all matters related to educational building. The planning and design of educational facilities has an impact on educational outcomes which is significant but hard to quantify. Building and running those facilities accounts for a substantial part of public educational expenditure in OECD countries. PEB's mission is to ensure that the maximum educational benefit is obtained from past and future investment in educational buildings and equipment, and that building stock is planned and managed in the most efficient way.

The Programme has three objectives:

- Improve the quality and suitability of educational buildings.
- Ensure that the best use is made of the resources devoted to planning, building, running and maintaining educational buildings.
- Give early warning of the impact on educational building of trends in education and in society as a whole.

The Programme's work is conducted through a set of activities determined by its member countries, and this third edition of the *PEB Compendium of Exemplary Educational Facilities* reflects concerns that PEB addressed during its 2002-06 Programme of Work.

See the Compendium site at www.oecd.org/edu/facilities/compendium. Further information about PEB is available at www.oecd.org/edu/facilities.

VASCONCELOS
l.i.b.r.a.r.y

"Vasconcelos library is one of the most impressive ones that I've visited in the world"

Kotchiro Matsuura
Director-General of UNESCO

mexico

asconcelos library aims to allow a larger umber of Mexicans free access to formation and knowledge. It collaborates ith and offers access to other libraries in exico and throughout the world, thereby romoting equitable lifelong development.

This is the largest modern library in Latin America. It has the capacity to store up to 1.5 million volumes and serves 6,520 users. The building has 6,000 seating spaces and 520 public access computers. It also houses language laboratories, two museums, a music hall, a children's library, an auditorium, an e-Mexico digital community centre and a media hall.

Structured as a beehive it is possible to add shelves reaching a full capacity of 1,750,000 books. Even though it is currently ready to accommodate a little more than 800,000 books. The site takes advantage of natural sunlight, thanks to its south-north orientation refurnished with blinds in order to protect the books.

- Special Mentions
- Multiple Levels
- Pre-primary and Primary Level
- Secondary Level
- Tertiary Level

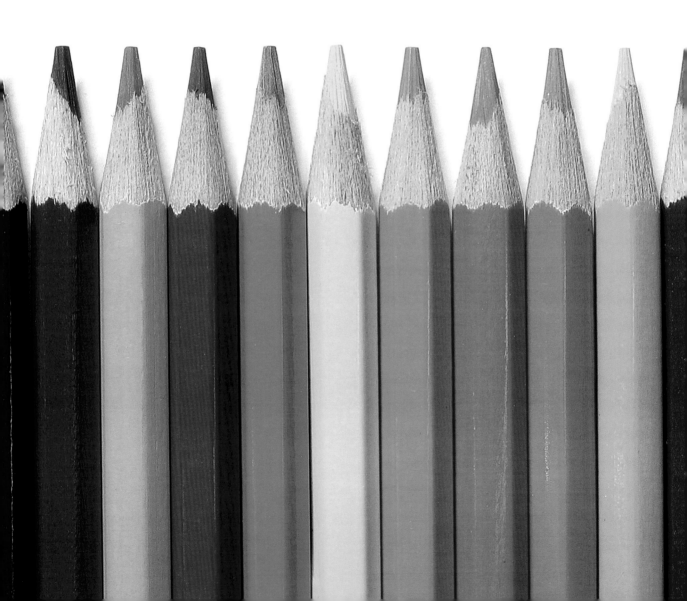

Fawood Children's Centre

London, United Kingdom (England)

Fawood Children's Centre
London, United Kingdom
(England)

Criteria
Flexibility / Community /
Sustainability / Security

Architect
Alan Lai, Alsop Design Ltd.

Type of School
Pre-primary

No. of Students
45/capacity for 75

Type of Project
New building

Gross Surface Area
1 600 m2

Year of Completion
2004

Client
Stonebridge Housing
Action Trust

"A very child-friendly environment – a colourful 'playbox' for dreaming and learning."

The bright and colourful Fawood Children's Centre in north-west London is a groundbreaking design venture for the education of young children, and reflects current thinking about how environments can affect learning. The Children's Centre initiative is based on the concept that providing integrated services for children and families that are locally based and easily accessible will result in long term benefits for all.

Integrated services, imaginative spaces

The Centre houses a state-of-the-art nursery combined with office space and training facilities to offer early education integrated with day care, family support and outreach to parents including child and family health services, and access to training and career opportunities.

The imaginative use of open spaces, with an emphasis on natural light and visual harmony, creates a child-friendly environment – a colourful "playbox" for dreaming and learning. Project architect Alan Lai of Alsop Design faced the challenge of creating a space not only to meet the needs of the children inside, but to also provide an enduring bright spot for the surrounding community. The local area was undergoing large-scale regeneration and the council wanted a focus for the community which would be visually exciting. Fundamental to the design was a desire to provide an environment that supports choice for children, includes space to socialise, builds confidence and enables independent learning. In keeping with this ethos, the Centre was built using recycled sea containers, which are linked by wooden decking and warmed by under floor heating.

Safety concerns

The local community and parents view the Centre as safe and secure, a main concern for those parents involved in the initial planning process. Ines Djeridi, who has a four-year-old daughter at the Centre says, "It's a very child-friendly building and the security is great. It's like a theme park and gives the children plenty of opportunity to get lots of exercise."

The innovative use of mesh walls to cover and protect the open air play areas creates a colourful social space for development and a decorative focal point for the community. As another parent explains, "When I first saw it I thought it was a bit unusual, but since my son has been coming here I see how practical the design is. The children are out in the fresh air without actually being outside."

Fawood Children's Centre

London, United Kingdom (England)

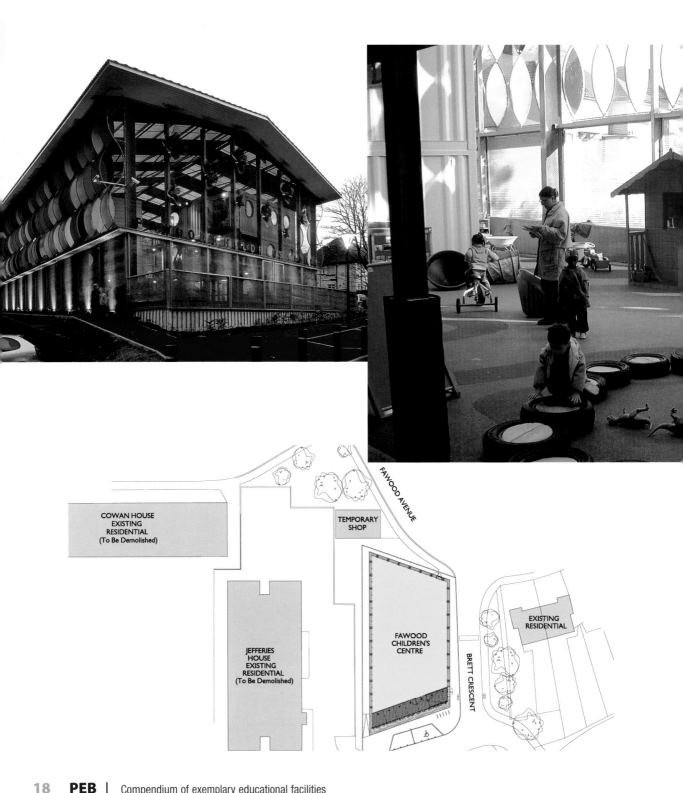

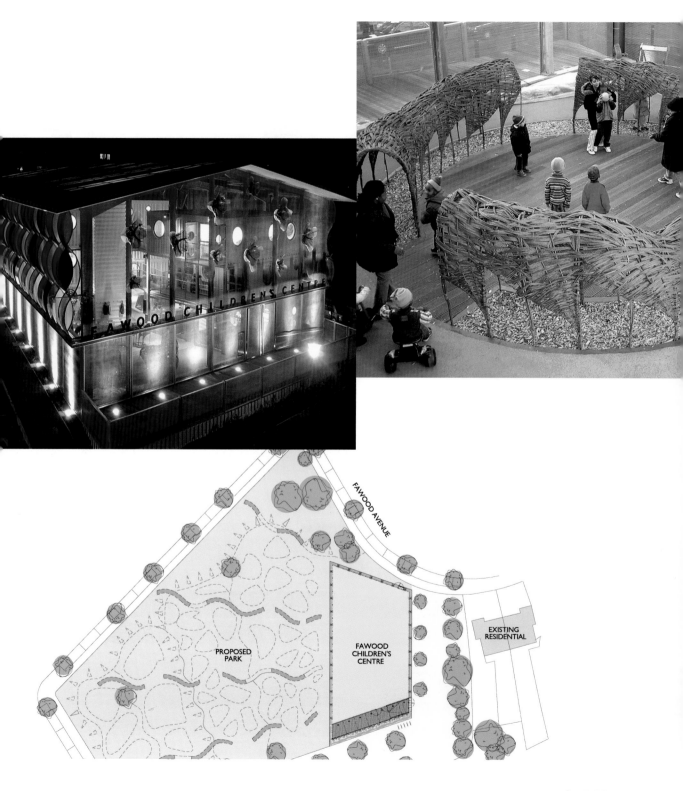

FAWOOD CHILDREN'S CENTRE

FAWOOD AVENUE

PROPOSED
PARK

FAWOOD
CHILDREN'S
CENTRE

EXISTING
RESIDENTIAL

Hampden Gurney Church of England Primary School

London, United Kingdom (England)

Hampden Gurney Church of England Primary School
London, United Kingdom (England)

Criteria
Flexibility / Security / Finance

Architect
Anthony McGuirk, Building Design Partnership

Type of School
Pre-primary and primary

No. of Students
220

Type of Project
New building

Gross Surface Area
4 400 m2

Year of Completion
2002

Client
Hampden Gurney Board of Trustees and Jarvis Construction

Hampden Gurney School is a new example of regeneration for urban schools. The creative approach taken to financing the project, by selling part of the land for the construction of 52 residential apartments on the site, funded the construction cost of the school building. This innovative design idea maximised a tight urban site, and resulted in a truly inspirational cornerpiece of urban regeneration.

The "vertical school"

Since the residential blocks took up much of the original play area, the challenge for the design team was to maintain the statutory amount of play area in a six-storey school. Building Design Partnership developed the concept of the multi-level "vertical school", where classrooms and play decks inter-relate learning and play with each classroom pair being linked across a light and ventilation well. The result is more play and teaching space of which the school could make more use on less than a third of the site.

In this vertical school, or "children's tower", students "move up" the school as they progress through the years. The school has been created over six levels, with the classrooms on three levels above the new ground floor nursery, a state-of-the-art library and multimedia room on other levels, and a group teaching room on the roof. The classrooms on each level are linked to open air play decks which provide safe weather-proof play and territory for each age group, accessed by a bridge across the central light well. The design also offers good north light for each classroom and the prospect of open air classes on warm days.

All the classrooms are naturally ventilated utilising the stack effect of the central light well. Close attention was paid to maximising available natural daylighting, and heating is kept to simple and cost effective systems to ensure that running costs are kept low and maintenance minimal.

Maximising its physical aspect

The location gives the school the best aspect for sunlight and a prominence within its neighbourhood. This deliberately outward looking building recognises the trustees' aspirations for it to play an active role in the social life of the community. Its height and innovative design gives it physical presence amongst its high neighbouring buildings whilst the staff and pupils enjoy a new prospect over their location.

Hampden Gurney Church of England Primary School

London, United Kingdom (England)

"Very good use of a tight site, and a creative approach to financing. Excellent outdoor play spaces at all levels."

CLASS 3

LIBRARY

LOBBY

VOID

CLASS 4

VOID

PLAY GARDEN

LOBBY

Hosmarinpuisto School and Day Care Centre

Espoo, Finland

Hosmarinpuisto School and Day Care Centre
Espoo, Finland

Criteria
Flexibility / Community / Sustainability

Architect
Yrjö Suonto

Type of School
Pre-primary and primary

No. of Students
208

Type of Project
New building

Gross Surface Area
3 300 m2

Year of Completion
2005

Client
City of Espoo

This school is an extraordinary example of a flexible, multi-use building that combines ecological ideas and construction with local materials in a stunning design. Completed in 2005, the facility provides education and development programmes for up to 250 children and is also used extensively by the local community for various activities.

Linking flexible areas

The school and day care main facilities surround the courtyard on two floors so that classrooms, lounges and open workshops are connected to each other around the building and orientation is easy, with the yard and rooms on the opposite side always visible. The school and day care centre are straight in connection, and as the link space there are libraries, craft rooms and science classrooms for all users. It is possible to cross the courtyard by a covered gangway around the perimeter, or by a wood and glass bridge which links the school to the cafeteria and office spaces. Long exterior eaves provide shelter from rain and large canopies give safe space for playing on the sides of the building. The building itself, both skeleton and elevations, is built of wood and the concept is based on ecological ideas.

Community space

The courtyard is a common space for all the children to socialise and learn. It is a play yard, but there are also gardens to take care of, a rainwater well and demonstrations of a solar energy system in use. The children interact with excellent examples of energy and environmental conservation strategies.

The building is also a meeting place for the neighbourhood and includes flexible options for cultural events. In the evenings the cafeteria, craft rooms and gymnasium are used by the local community. The gymnasium has a stage with modern audiovisual equipment and it can be connected to the cafeteria with sliding doors. Bigger events like annual ceremonies and concerts are also possible to organise when the doors to the impressive courtyard are opened in summertime.

Hosmarinpuisto School and Day Care Centre
Espoo, Finland

SPORTS PARK

STORE

DA

PLAYING YARD

"Stunning design. The use of local materials offers flexibility."

YARD

L

HOUSING AREA

YARD

MAIN ENTRANCE

NER YARD
RIUM

PARKING

HOUSING AREA

Rudolf Steinerschool

Leuven, Belgium

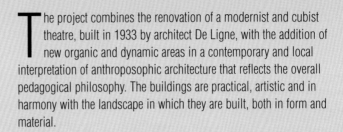

Rudolf Steinerschool
Leuven, Belgium

Criteria
Flexibility / Community / Sustainability/
Security / Finance

Architect
ABCD (Architects Bekker,
Carnoy and Deru)

Type of School
Primary and lower secondary

No. of Students
360

Type of Project
New building

Gross Surface Area
4 400 m2

Year of Completion
2000

Client
VZW Rudolf Steinerschool

The project combines the renovation of a modernist and cubist theatre, built in 1933 by architect De Ligne, with the addition of new organic and dynamic areas in a contemporary and local interpretation of anthroposophic architecture that reflects the overall pedagogical philosophy. The buildings are practical, artistic and in harmony with the landscape in which they are built, both in form and material.

A connecting spiral

The project is situated in a park area divided in three parts by linden alleys. These three parts are connected by a spiral footpath that provides the functional backbone of the project. This spiral ends up in the internal circulation and the arts tower where the music room and other workshops are located, while the main classrooms are located along the corridor forming part of the spiral. The renovated theatre offers expanded studio and art space.

Low impact construction

Energy efficiency is addressed through optimal isolation, orientation, use of natural light and controlled ventilation. The production of sustainable energy was not possible, but particular strategies such as the reuse of rainwater for lavatories and the application of rainwater in the layout of the playground are notable. The new building materials have little environmental impact in their production, application and use.

A group of teachers and parents worked together on all aspects of the project from the analysis, evaluation and elaboration of the building site to the architectural expression and concept, including issues of sustainability and choice of materials. The architects gave workshops in each class, where the children could draw, describe and model the school of their dreams. Inspired by these ideas, the architects provided the final and coherent synthesis.

The Steiner pedagogy offers a general education at primary and secondary level with a focus not only on acquisition of knowledge but also on artistic (music, dance, theatre, arts) and technical (crafts, gardening) development. "The new building shows harmony, a sprinkling of light and contact with the surrounding nature. The playing child, the growing up pupil and the developing adolescent have a full formation in this stimulating surrounding. The realisation of the project means an increase in value for the pedagogical project," explains the facilities manager.

Rudolf Steinerschool
Leuven, Belgium

"Welcoming and artistic, expressing well its educational function. Parent involvement, including fundraising, has resulted in an inspirational building."

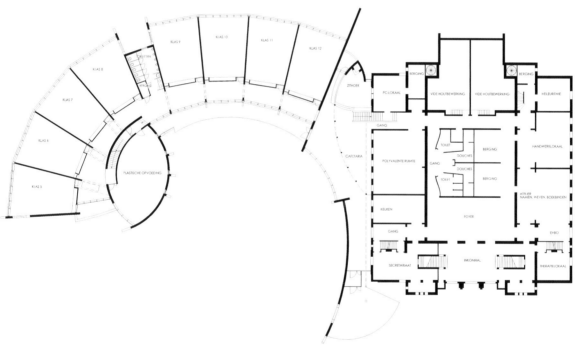

Vikurskóli

Reykajvik, Iceland

Vikurskóli
Reykajvik, Iceland

Criteria
Flexibility / Community / Sustainability

Architect
Sigurdur Gústafsson

Type of School
Primary and secondary
(lower and upper)

No. of Students
260

Type of Project
New building

Gross Surface Area
4 400 m2

Year of Completion
2003

Client
Framkvaemdasvid Reykjavíkurborgar

This state-of-the-art school is designed to be the centrepiece of its community and is located in the middle of the neighbourhood. Its various units are placed along a "main street" linking the building units, open areas, playgrounds and parks of the surrounding neighbourhood. All the services and facilities required by this small community can be found on the street.

Individualised and inclusive education

Each age group has its own building on the street. Some of the classrooms are 120 m2 and can be divided into workstations for flexible teaching plans. All classrooms and open areas are easily connected to the Internet. It is also easy to move televisions, laptop boxes and other technical equipment. There are no closed areas or corners, which also makes supervision of students easier. The main idea is to have a building suitable for individualised and inclusive education.

The social area, dining/assembly hall, recreation room, library and kindergarten are all in the same core space with good interconnecting access. The music room is also connected to this core. Two sail-shaped walls, clad with Korten steel, are a feature of the assembly hall. The library and the computer room are in the middle. The kindergarten faces the garden and is connected to the dining room and other social spaces. The elliptical garden, complete with play equipment, is an ideal outdoor area.

Traditional building techniques

The building is constructed from concrete and the roof over the main corridor is constructed from laminated wood. The classrooms are clad with unpainted, galvanised, corrugated iron sheeting. The curved wall across the main corridor, like the sail-shaped walls of the assembly hall, is clad with Korten steel. The low wall that faces the garden is a turf covered, dry-stone wall that softens the southern aspect and demonstrates traditional Icelandic building techniques to the children.

The school grounds and building are designed in an environmentally friendly way. The electricity comes from water power plants and the building is heated by thermal water from the earth. The whole building has an energy saving system. The natural aspect of the school is outstanding for environmental education.

Vikurskóli
Reykajvik, Iceland

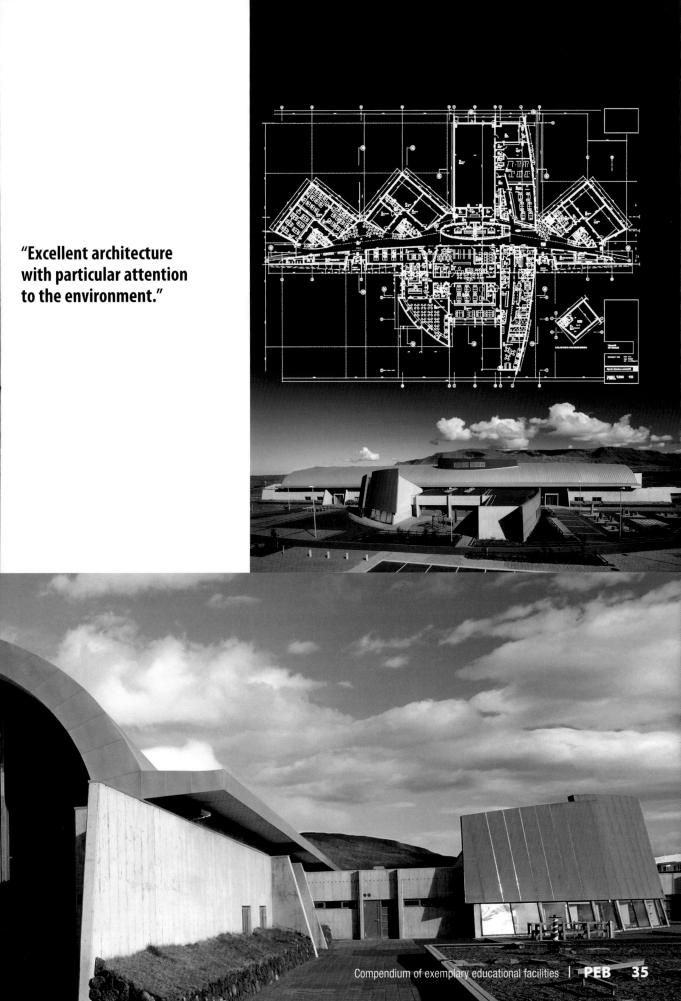

"Excellent architecture with particular attention to the environment."

Fukushima Prefectural Koriyama School for the Physically Handicapped

Fukushima, Japan

Fukushima Prefectural Koriyama School for the Physically Handicapped
Fukushima, Japan

Criteria
Flexibility / Sustainability

Architect
Kazuo Watabe, Yui Architects & Planners

Type of School
Primary and secondary
(lower and upper)

No. of Students
170

Type of Project
New building

Gross Surface Area
13 525 m2

Year of Completion
2001

Client
Fukushima Prefecture

This is a combined elementary and secondary school for children with physical disabilities. The architecture is designed to allow younger and older children of the different grades to mix, while maintaining close relationships among children of the same grade. Each classroom is small with only three to eight students, but as children move from a workspace to a playroom and on to the gymnasium, they can increase the size of their group in phases at will, making it possible for them to develop a variety of flexible human relationships.

Appealing to all five senses

The space of this school is structured so that the children enjoy a sequence of dramatic changes as they move from one room to another. Children move to the next space as if they were being led by sunlight through light wells and high sidelights. For children in wheelchairs, the spiral slope is not just a facility for descending or ascending, it also provides mental comfort and pleasure while moving within the school.

Users of the building point out that, thanks to the well thought out layout which makes the school bright even in winter, the children have become more active. In addition, the barrier-free design creates a seamless activity area from the inside to the outside of the architecture, appealing to the five senses of the children. The transparent partitions between classrooms and corridors allow children to see what programme is going on in each classroom, further enhancing their desire to participate.

To understand the diversified needs of children with disabilities and address them in the design, the firm of Yui Architects & Planners held a workshop with end-users. The discussion of ideas included pictures, poems, models, and other items created and presented by the children under the title "My Ideal School", and helped greatly to come up with a specific image of the architecture. The result is a safe, active and open learning environment that combines these ideas with an exceptional architectural concept to create a very special educational facility.

Fukushima Prefectural Koriyama School for the Physically Handicapped
Fukushima, Japan

"Provides excellent, safe learning environment with innovative circulation."

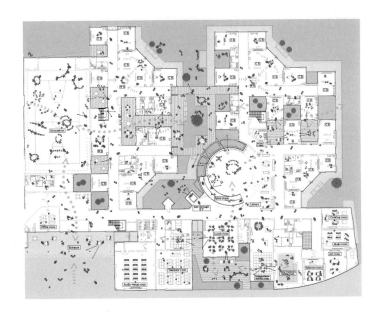

Canning Vale College

Perth, Australia

Canning Vale College
Perth, Australia

Criteria
Flexibility / Community / Sustainability

Architect
HASSELL

Type of School
Lower and upper secondary

No. of Students
1 200

Type of Project
Extension

Gross Surface Area
13 000 m2

Year of Completion
Stage one – 2004
Stage two to be completed 2007

Client
Western Australia Department of
Education and Training

The way in which students learn is being challenged and is evolving at a rapid pace. The design process for Canning Vale College was driven by educational thinking and a collaborative approach to imagining how students might best learn now, and in the future.

Putting children first

Stage one, completed in 2004, included a lower secondary school, a library, and performing arts and specialist facilities, and was developed from a series of ten guiding principles established in collaboration with educators and the community with the overall vision of "putting children first". Design innovations developed specifically for this stage include:

- A wetland "living stream" learning resource.
- "Solar chimney" passive ventilating elements.
- Large pivoting display wall panels that change layout of space for different modes of teaching.
- Wireless networking systems throughout the school.
- A fabric roofed street area between the library and a combined specialist services building.
- Instead of four normal sized classrooms, a large learning area the size of five classrooms to provide flexibility for any teaching style or technique.

Stage two, currently under construction, continues this collaboration between the school community, education experts and the architect. An upper secondary "senior" school will be linked to the lower secondary school by a covered "learning street" of specialist, cross-curricula facilities.

The senior school building further develops the educational vision and responds to the needs of more mature learners with a two-storey office building archetype. Peter Rudrum, CVC Associate Principal Senior School, describes the schematic design, "The senior school campus has been designed for students in the late adolescent phase of schooling who want a major role in determining the decisions that affect their lives and their learning experiences. They require a flexible curriculum and flexible learning spaces that provide the opportunity for them to demonstrate a high level of responsibility in the management of their own learning. Social spaces for informal gatherings are important to them. They want a building that welcomes them and announces that they are entering an 'adult learning environment', which meets all their needs. The atrium entrance statement will set the tone of an adult learning culture and the inhabited ramp and courtyard will provide a focal point for both formal and informal meeting places."

Canning Vale College

Perth, Australia

"Student-centred. An excellent flexible design which will respond well to future changes."

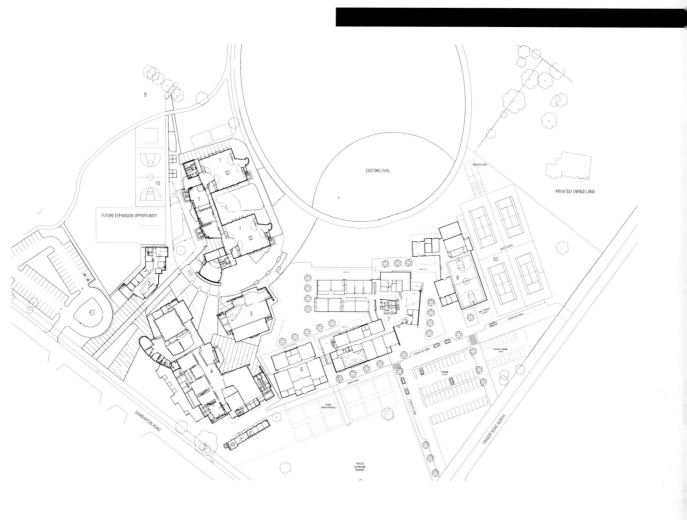

Kingsdale School

London, United Kingdom (England)

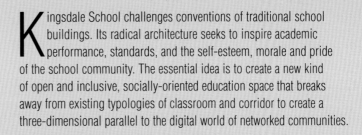

Kingsdale School
London, United Kingdom
(England)

Criteria
Flexibility / Community

Architect
dRMM Architects

Type of School
Secondary (lower and upper)
and tertiary

No. of Students
1 200

Type of Project
Extension (reconstruction)

Gross Surface Area
5 000 m2

Year of Completion
2006

Client
Southwark Education

Kingsdale School challenges conventions of traditional school buildings. Its radical architecture seeks to inspire academic performance, standards, and the self-esteem, morale and pride of the school community. The essential idea is to create a new kind of open and inclusive, socially-oriented education space that breaks away from existing typologies of classroom and corridor to create a three-dimensional parallel to the digital world of networked communities.

An inspiring mixed-use space

Various design interventions feature a number of "firsts"; most notably what appears to be the world's largest "variable skin" ETFE roof enclosure. This exploits the potential of the existing 1960s building, superimposing a translucent light-controlling membrane over a redefined and column-free 3 200 m2 internal courtyard. Within this open space, the largest ever created in a British school, free access to facilities is encouraged beyond the curriculum and timetable within one inspiring mixed-use space.

Existing access is further improved by new walkways, a lift and a bridge. Aerial walkways connect stairs and reduce corridors, providing sightlines and seating. The focal point of the complex is a spectacular timber geodesic assembly/performance/cinema auditorium above a school library. This marks the new heart of the school with a clearly defined iconic facility.

Improving academic performance

Historically, Kingsdale was regarded as a "sink" school with a bad reputation. Since the project began, and particularly since the main sections of the refurbishment were completed, pupil recruitment and retention have steadily improved. Students like the building, the space, its colours and interest. As a consequence, morale and student behaviour have improved, while vandalism and staff turnover have reduced.

The Kingsdale School Works consultation project has involved the whole extended school community in ongoing critiques of the existing and proposed building designs. This collaboration took the form of interviews, presentations, workshops, seminars, student projects, questionnaires and a great many meetings, which continue today. This means a close and detailed fit between the building and user needs wherever work has been carried out. "We asked de Rijke Marsh Morgan for a plane, they gave us Concorde," says the head teacher Steve Morrison.

Kingsdale School
London, United Kingdom (England)

classrooms   dining   auditorium   assembly   classrooms

etfe roof

"Inspirational and innovative transformation of an existing school. Pupil involvement in the project will contribute undoubtedly to sustaining dramatic improvements in attainment levels."

HEC Montréal
Montreal, Canada

HEC Montréal
Montreal, Canada

Criteria
Flexibility / Community / Sustainability

Architect
Dan S. Hanganu, Jodoin, Lamarre, Pratte et Associés

Type of School
Tertiary

No. of Students
5 834 full time, 5 984 part time

Type of Project
Renovation

Gross Surface Area
76 001 m2

Year of Completion
2005

Client
HEC Montréal

W ith its majestic façade, state-of-the-art technology, dynamic learning environment and commitment to low impact construction, *HEC Montréal* is a role model for educational facilities worldwide.

Active and dynamic

The distinctive modern columns at the main entrance to HEC express the commitment and determination to provide the highest quality education inside. The library, bathed in natural light through great windows and open spaces, is an active and dynamic learning space, an environment designed to be conducive to study and research. It is also the largest library of its kind in Canada and is regarded as one of the most important bilingual management libraries in the world.

HEC Montréal is equipped with a 10 gigabits network. Its architecture is recognised as one of the best networks in North America. More than 420 km of copper cables and fibre optics line the building walls, and 10 000 network connections are scattered throughout the classrooms, library, work rooms and common areas, that allow the use of portable computers and Internet access from virtually anywhere in the building.

The classrooms are equipped with network connections at each student and teacher station, and there are six computer laboratories, one of which is accessible around the clock, seven days a week.

Exceptional technology supports the HEC trading room, one of the largest and best equipped in the university world. A trading environment with simulations for teaching and training purposes are organised and made possible through the exceptional technological applications.

"Never before in Canada has an organisation, a company or a municipality gone as far as *HEC Montréal* to preserve a wooded area surrounding a building. The school is nothing less than a leader in this field," states Luc Nadeau, a forestry engineer at Foreso Inc., an engineering firm whose chief specialisation is trees in urban settings.

"Until now, only a few organisations in the United States had ever taken such measures to protect flora in urban areas. *HEC Montréal* is a forerunner and its building project is a veritable laboratory that people are already citing as a model," concludes Mr. Nadeau.

HEC Montréal
Montreal, Canada

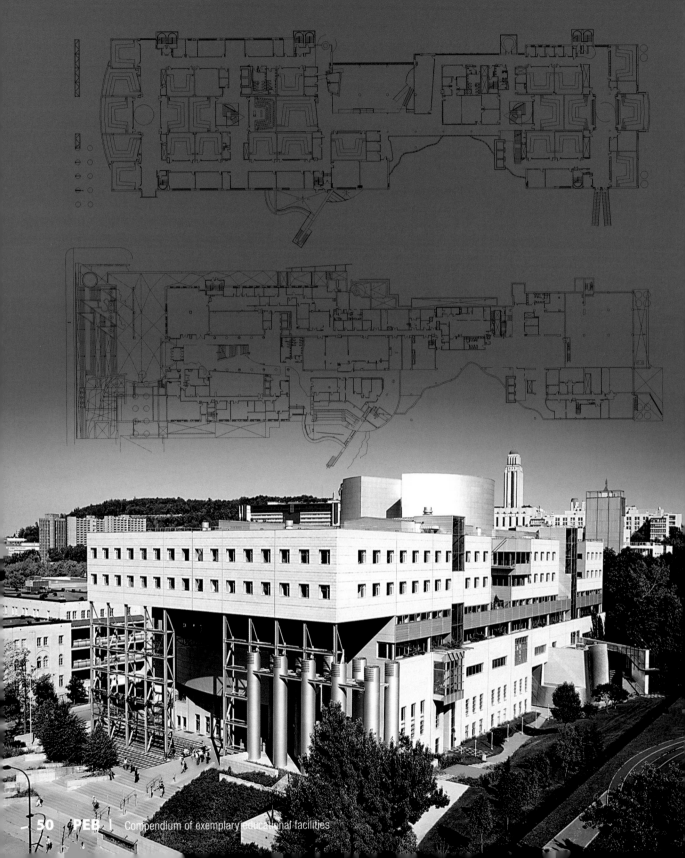

"Great sense of student enjoyment. Architectural design with character."

City of Westminster College
Paddington Learning Centre
25 Paddington Green
London W2 1NB

Building the Future on Knowledge

Education has always played an important role in preparing students for success in work and life. But now it's also seen as the critical path to enable nations to compete in a rapidly changing, knowledge-based global economy. There's increasing pressure to improve educational quality and outcomes. At the same time, there's an opportunity to inspire the next generation. Technology in primary and secondary school classrooms has emerged as a key strategy to take education to a new level—one that will enable a future built on knowledge.

Information and communications technology (ICT) is now recognized as an essential ingredient for creating 21st century learning environments that engage learners with student-centered approaches, dynamic digital curriculum, and the freedom to go beyond textbooks and classroom walls. The current challenge is identifying and implementing the best methods and solutions, so that your investment in technology delivers measurable value for the future.

The roadmap to 21st century learning

To be competitive in today's knowledge economy, students need to develop new learning skills. They need to become knowledge creators— independent learners equipped and motivated for lifelong learning. As the classroom environment evolves, they can evolve with it, moving from knowledge acquisition (facts and memorization) to knowledge deepening (open-ended questions and cross-subject application), and finally, to knowledge creation.

Whether you're introducing or expanding ICT in your schools, successful implementation takes several key components working together. Strong technology platforms, connectivity, professional development, improved teaching and learning methods, and digital curriculum all contribute to an environment where 21st century skills flourishes and students thrive.

What are 21st century learning skills?

- o Technology and media literacy
- o Effective communication
- o Critical thinking
- o Problem solving
- o Collaboration

Our role goes far beyond the chip

Intel brings to the table a unique combination of capabilities to help transform learning environments. Our innovative technology platforms, collaboration with a wide range of experts, and deep commitment to educational issues and programs enable schools to leap into 21st century learning.

Working with educators, governments, and industry leaders around the world, Intel is helping to develop and document the best ways to use and implement ICT for improved teaching and learning including issues such as professional development, digital curriculum, and evaluating outcomes.

The Intel® Education initiative is Intel's large-scale commitment to accelerate 21st century education for the knowledge economy. We cooperate with governments and educators around the world to help improve teaching and learning through the effective use of technology, and to advance math, science, and engineering education and research.

Intel's corporate social responsibility programs represent an investment of more than $1 billion (USD) in 50 countries, and are recognized by governments and international organizations for their positive impact on education.

Programs such as Intel® Teach to the Future, Intel® Learn, and the Intel Computer Clubhouse Network help educators effectively use technology to enhance students' 21st century learning skills. Intel advances science and engineering education and research through sponsorship of the Intel International Science and Engineering Fair and the Intel Science Talent Search. In addition, through the Intel® Higher Education Program, we work with more than 100 universities in 30 countries to advance technology innovation and develop a pipeline of technical talent.

For more information, please visit   http://www.intel.com/education

The Community School of Auchterarder

United Kingdom (Scotland)

The Community School of Auchterarder
United Kingdom (Scotland)

Criteria

Flexibility / Community / Security

Architect

Anderson Bell + Christie

Type of School

Pre-primary, primary and secondary
(lower and upper)

No. of Students

1 078

Type of Project

New building

Gross Surface Area

13 055 m2

Year of Completion

2004

Client

Perth and Kinross Council

The Community School of Auchterarder reflects a commitment to continuous improvement and an inclusive, responsible and progressive vision. A key policy objective guiding the project design was to create a campus environment conducive to evolving teaching strategies, national priorities, learning experiences and curriculum requirements that would not only raise educational attainment standards, but also become the very heart of the surrounding community.

Traditional methods, modern vision

The buildings clearly express their function as a place of learning, and are attractive and positive. The design has made reference to the original townscape structure of Auchterarder with roof forms derived from the surrounding farm architecture as well as local natural stone laid using local methods. The building's masterplan has interpreted the *feu*, a traditional narrow building plot, in a modern way so that the buildings make an appropriate intervention and create a distinctive sense of place unique to Auchterarder.

The campus has been designed to be an integral part of the community and presents an open and welcoming face to the smaller surrounding villages as well. Facilities such as the library and sports hall have been grouped into a community and administration hub building. This allows these facilities to be used in a managed way by both students and members of the community.

Numerous open spaces

The layout of the primary school is such that a sequence of courtyards is formed in between the buildings to provide secure external play space for the children. These spaces are sheltered by large roof overhangs and contain a number of play and educational elements designed in collaboration with artists.

The primary school classrooms are arranged in a semi-open plan configuration with additional "breakout" spaces and "quiet rooms" divided by specially designed storage walls. Art, music and drama specialist areas are also provided.

The secondary school classrooms open onto a large double height covered atrium. The street acts as circulation space as well as a social space for the building. The classrooms have been canted to add interest both to the side elevations and to the atrium. The entire facility is designed to provide a flexible environment which will continue to meet future needs.

Türk Eğitim Derneği (TED) Ankara Koleji

Ankara, Turkey

Students feel the flexibility of the space and can follow the natural circle of the seasons with natural building materials. The transparency of the spaces encourages them to disclose their abilities, and the use of light makes them warm and open.

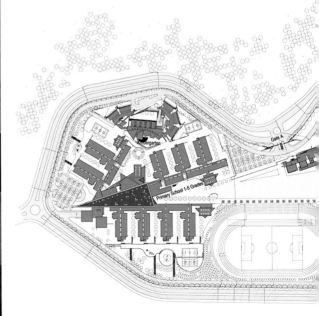

Türk Eğitim Derneği (TED)
Ankara Koleji
Ankara, Turkey

Criteria
Flexibility / Community

Architect
Semra Uygur, Özcan Uygur, Uygur
Mimarlik Ltd.

Type of School
Pre-primary, primary and secondary
(lower and upper)

No. of Students
5 499

Type of Project
New building

Gross Surface Area
141 000 m2

Year of Completion
2003 through 2005

Client
Türk Eğitim Derneği (TED)

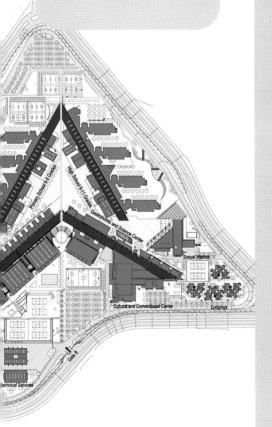

W ith a land area of 309 000 m2 and a campus expanding to 141 000 m2, TED Ankara College is internationally known for its student capacity and facilities for close to 6 000 teachers, students and visitors. The institution has always aimed to be a few steps ahead of traditional education concepts and strives to develop the imagination, creativity and spirit of exploration in its students.

A community centre

The campus has been designed to meet not only the educational aspects for kindergarten through secondary levels, but also to provide the community with athletic, social and cultural centres. This includes a sports hall for 3 000 people, swimming pools, tennis courts, squash, dance rooms, gymnasiums, a fitness center and sauna. There is also a shopping centre; an art centre with nine studios for various disciplines; a scientific centre for workshops and ongoing research; a spacious theatre-auditorium for 800 people; a cultural and conference centre consisting of a foyer area and six seminar halls; a TED museum; and a social club with a restaurant overlooking Lake Mogan.

The school is designed to meet the evolving needs of education in contemporary spaces and teaching modes. The physical infrastructure and technical facilities of the campus allow students to develop in creative, constructive and productive ways.

Urban aspect

The main design concepts promote the use of natural light with a sense of urban planning and living. Based on the idea of alleys and streets, the different sections are linked by spines forming internal courtyards used as recreation areas.

The large atrium at the junction of the arms leads to an amphitheatre that also invites students to interact in social activities. The orientation of the classroom clusters and the extensive use of glass in the roof give abundant natural light. This provides a calm and relaxed atmosphere and gives students a feeling of freedom. Easily accessible sport and multi-purpose workshop halls in each block offer flexibility and variety of use.

Mittelschule Carlbergergasse
Vienna, Austria

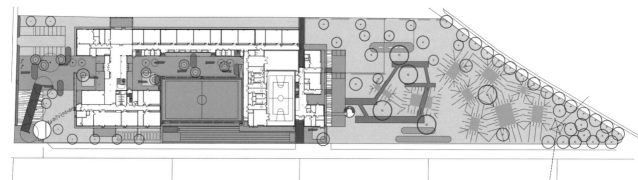

Mittelschule Carlbergergasse
Vienna, Austria

Criteria
Flexibility / Community / Finance

Architect
Johannes Zieser, zieserArchitekt

Type of School
Pre-primary and lower secondary

No. of Students
320

Type of Project
New building

Gross Surface Area
4 355 m2

Year of Completion
1994

Client
Provincial Government of Vienna

Situated on a large piece of land within a dense urban neighbourhood, the Carlbergergasse Junior High School, with its surrounding park-like recreational area for the young, provides an open green space and a bright, friendly ambience together with its outstanding curriculum.

The ambitious curriculum objectives within the school are mirrored in the facility's design. For the first time in Vienna's school building history, a hard court and courtyard were conjoined to a patio-like layout surrounded by the building wings. The project required energetic and efficient fundraising by all partners of the school, and the result attracts visitors from all over who want to learn about the exceptional education programme and visit the award winning building.

The principal of the school explains the functional benefits of the clearly arranged layout and design, "The space allocation plan and layout of all the rooms fits the needs of the school in an outstanding manner, especially those rooms which are designated for multi-purpose use. All the classrooms are well adapted for individual education and the open spaces in the facility are used in a very flexible way." The school's central courtyard offers an excellent example of a flexible open space where students can interact, play and learn.

The lower secondary school community and people from the surrounding neighbourhood use the school's unique and attractive facilities for sporting events, celebrations and festivals, private viewings, readings and concerts on a regular basis.

Seoul National School
for the Blind
Seoul, Korea

Seoul National School for the Blind
Seoul, Korea

Criteria
Community / Security

Architect
Dowoo Architects Associates Ltd.

Type of School
Pre-primary, primary,
secondary and tertiary

No. of Students
108

Type of Project
New building

Gross Surface Area
7 974 m2

Year of Completion
2004

Client
Seoul National School for the Blind

S eoul National School for the Blind is a special education facility
for students with blindness and visual impairment. Founded
by the Korean government, the school provides six distinct
educational programmes: a kindergarten, an elementary school, lower
and upper secondary schools, a vocational rehabilitation programme
for *iryo* (acupuncture, moxibustion and massages), and an advanced
vocational programme.

In addition to the national basic curriculum offered for kindergarten
through secondary school, there are courses for adaptive skills required
to overcome visual impairment. The upper secondary school programme
has two separate curricula, one for college-preparatory academic
courses and the other for *iryo* vocational courses.

To accommodate these and the two tertiary programmes, the building
includes not only classrooms, a library and a gymnasium, but also
vocational rehabilitation facilities and a training centre for the special
iryo curricula.

Facilitating circulation

A main feature of the building design is the convenient access to all
facilities and a one-way movement flow to facilitate circulation and
prevent students from having to navigate in opposite directions. The
layout weaves indoor and outdoor open spaces for an efficient use of the
site, and carefully incorporates an external courtyard for flexible teaching
opportunities and an informal meeting place for students.

Other important features of the facility include a fully equipped dormitory
for resident students separate from the educational space. There are also
facilities for specialist teaching in Braille, training in social skills and
physical education programmes. Finally, information technology
resources are adapted for student use, and safety and security systems
have been implemented with careful consideration.

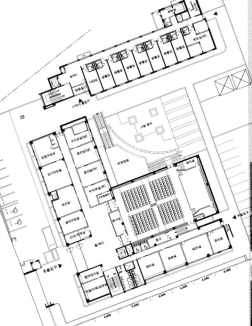

Arabian Peruskoulu
Helsinki, Finland

The whole building is a place for interaction.

Vision, communication, inclusion and satisfaction.

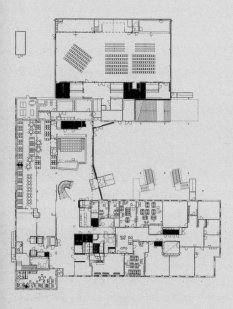

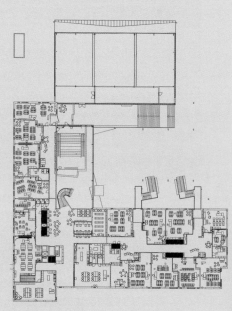

Arabian Peruskoulu
Helsinki, Finland

Criteria
Flexibility / Community / Sustainability

Architect
Vesa Peltonen + Wartiainen Archtects
(Evata Finland)

Type of School
Primary and lower secondary

No. of Students
360

Type of Project
Renovation

Gross Surface Area
5 754 m2

Year of Completion
2003

Client
City of Helsinki Education Department

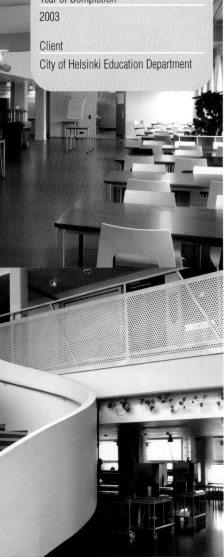

The Arabia Comprehensive School, located in the Arabianranta area of Helsinki, provides primary and lower secondary classes for 18 basic education and three special education groups, with additional multicultural and co-operative programmes. The study programme emphasises the arts, as well as environment and natural science studies.

Building ideas into action

In considering the design and construction of the school, the members of the working group focused on four main themes: vision, communication, inclusion and satisfaction. It was also important to combine the highest quality architecture with economic viability, and to provide an educational facility that would also effectively serve the surrounding community.

The school building is divided into small units with the classrooms and other working spaces all connected. There are glass walls for interaction. In each unit there are flexible options for group work, social activities and other multifunctional uses. The extensive use of glass in the school building guarantees the safety inside: you can always see, you can always be seen, and the working environment is open and communicative for both children and adults. The whole building is a place for interaction.

The school building should always respect its educational function. Particularly in developing urban areas, the first class architecture of a school building like the Arabian Comprehensive School provides an important function by offering a sense of identity. It is a building to be shared and enjoyed by the whole neighbourhood.

Aurinkolahden Peruskoulu

Helsinki, Finland

Multifunctional central space is the core of the school.

Aurinkolahden Peruskoulu
Helsinki, Finland

Criteria
Flexibility / Community / Finance

Architect
Jeskanen-Repo-Teränne Arkkitehdit Oy
and Arkkitehtitoimisto Leena
Yli-Lonttinen Ky

Type of School
Primary and lower secondary

No. of Students
540

Type of Project
New building

Gross Surface Area
6 370 m2

Year of Completion
2002

Client
City of Helsinki Education Department

I n 1999, the City of Helsinki Education Department and the Finnish Constructional Steel Association organised an open architectural competition for a school building of the future, based on a new interactive pedagogy and developing the use of steel structures and new technology in school buildings. The Aurinkolahti Comprehensive School is developed from the winning entry from among the 100 submissions.

The focus of the design is to provide an environment that promotes learning and a sense of community among children. Special attention was given to providing spaces for different kinds of teamwork and social activities. The school is exceptionally well equipped with new technology, both IT and stagecraft. The school is also designed to fully meet the challenges of educating pupils with special needs.

Cell units around a central hub

The essential architectural idea is a three-storey central space with glass walls that creates a multi-functional, visual and circulation hub for the school, and provides the heart of the building. The central space is surrounded by two-storey-high units, organised as cells. Each cell has its own colour, indicating a smaller unit within the whole school. The classrooms are organised around teamwork areas. The school's educational focus is technology education and cognitive learning. Educational technology is used to help create a community of learners who build knowledge together.

The feedback from the users has been very positive. According to principal Tuula Matikainen, the facilities meet the needs of the users and they are especially happy with the central space. "It functions very well as a social and circulation point. The cell solution for the classrooms also functions well in the day-to-day school life, as the design reduces noise, and the glass walls in the classrooms are very useful in creative teaching situations." With a definitive design and outstanding facilities that enhance learning, it is truly a school for the future.

Collège « L'Esplanade »

Begnins, Switzerland

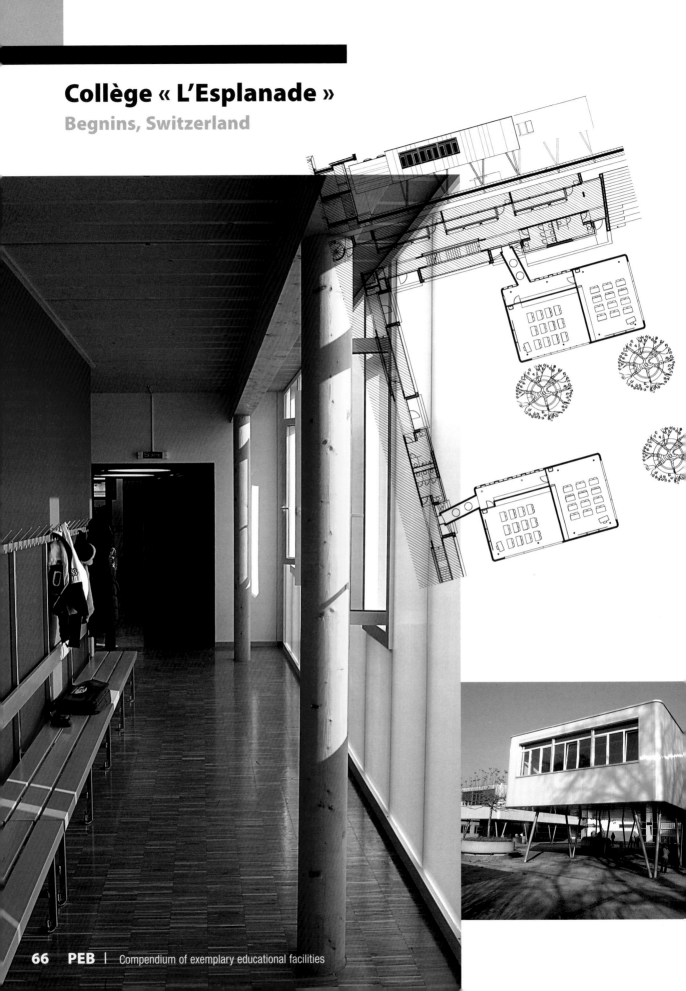

Collège « L'Esplanade »
Begnins, Switzerland

Criteria
Flexibility/Security

Architect
Pascal de Benoit & Martin Wagner
Architectes, S.A.

Type of School
Primary and lower secondary

No. of Students
750

Type of Project
New building

Gross Surface Area
450 m2

Year of Completion
2003

Client
Commune de Begnins

The addition of four supplementary classrooms at the *Collège « L'Esplanade »* required a careful use of the existing space. By elevating the new classrooms, the architects have created a modern, flexible and inventive dimension to the school as a whole. This simple and elegant solution has transformed the structure and use of the school building inside and out.

Architectural and functional improvement

The new classrooms have been placed in two separate wings of two classrooms each. The wings are easily linked to the upper floors of the main building, without any interruption to the flow or operation of the school. Wood was used as the primary material for the frame and interior panelling because of its economic efficiency, rapid construction, and the sense of warmth and well-being it brings to the classrooms. An impermeable coating of translucent polycarbonate and fire-proof aluminium sheeting covers the exterior.

The elevated wings extend into the courtyard, adding varied play areas to the existing space without sacrificing the surface area. The wings are like space shuttles moored by a gangway/airlock to the school's main structure. The unique form and appearance of the wings brings a modern aspect to the school while providing much needed classroom space. The simple solution was constructed in 15 days and fully functional in two months. Economy of space, elegant simplicity and integration of energetic concepts all combine in this eye-catching design and construction.

Escola E.B.I./J.I. da Malagueira

Évora, Portugal

The architectural
option chosen for
this school is an
ideal solution given
the initial goals of
the project.

Escola E.B.I./J.I. da Malagueira
Évora, Portugal

Criteria
Flexibility / Community

Architect
Farelo Pinto, Gabinete
de Arquitectura, Lta.

Type of School
Pre-primary, primary and lower
secondary

No. of Students
646

Type of Project
New building

Gross Surface Area
9 471 m2

Year of Completion
2004

Client
Regional Department of Education of
Alentejo - Ministry of Education

The main idea behind this project is to foster the fullest possible integration of young people from different backgrounds and abilities in a dynamic and vibrant learning environment, and to ensure that all of the existing educational resources are used to promote mutual sharing across diverse age groups, helping children to interact and develop social skills.

Integrating design

The physical layout of the school is designed to provide a continuous link between pre-school education and each of the higher levels. All the specialised education areas such as the library, auditorium, music rooms, computer rooms and refectory have been designed for shared use. The architectural concept of the project is intended to accommodate pupils from ages 3 to 15 in a physical environment that promotes social inclusion and diversity.

A key objective of the school is to facilitate the early integration of young children from an urban area in the city of Évora. The location was chosen mainly to take in pupils from a range of different areas and social classes. The education, adaptation and social development of these students are enhanced by the open and welcoming environment and structure of the school. The curriculum includes opportunities for students to experiment with art, dance, music, theatre and new technologies right from pre-school age, and to develop important learning and social skills as they progress through the school programme.

The architecture chosen for this school is an ideal solution given the initial goals of the project. The use of colour, space and natural elements enhance the outdoor social spaces, while the fully enclosed school building creates a sense of community and inclusion. The pupils and staff at different levels have already made substantial progress in terms of social interaction and the shared use of the facilities. The school also has a class of deaf pupils who have successfully integrated into the structure and organisation of the school without any problem.

Lækjarskóli
Hafnarfjörður, Iceland

The entire Lækjarskóli facility promotes individual development and social interaction in an exceptional environment.

Lækjarskóli
Hafnarfjörðaur, Iceland

Criteria
Flexibility / Community / Sustainability

Architect
Á Stofunni

Type of School
Primary and lower secondary

No. of Students
550

Type of Project
New building

Gross Surface Area
6 800 m2

Year of Completion
2003

Client
Nytak

Lækjarskóli is a long established school located in the centre of Hafnarfjörðaur. As a centrepiece for the community, situated within a protected nature area, it was important for the new school building to incorporate appropriate design elements and materials. A main objective of the project is to create a learning environment that promotes Lækjarskóli's three basic principles of respect, responsibility and safety, and to facilitate the inclusion of special needs students into mainstream classes.

An essential issue

The environment became an essential issue in the design of the new school. The school's spectacular surroundings called for a unique design with special visual and aesthetic aspects. The main materials, especially the wood and stone, were selected to reflect the local environment. Large windows were used so that people inside the building can enjoy the beautiful lava rock formations and a small stream outside.

The building is open and spacious, bright and well lit. The colours represent the flora around the site and give each part a certain identity relating to the different age groups. It is a linear building on two floors with three transverse wings that cut through the building. Connecting the main areas of the school is a "road" where students and staff circulate and interact, creating continuous movement and activity. Student artwork is on display in this social area as well.

Meeting student needs

Lækjarskóli has three special units: a unit for students 6 to 12 years with special needs, a multicultural unit for foreign students of all ages, and a unit for 15- and 16-year-olds that focuses on learning and behavioural difficulties. The new building incorporates the first two units, uniting these diverse groups in a facility uniquely designed to provide individualised curricula in an open, unified environment with flexible shared use spaces. The school also offers a "culture hall" for community events and larger social activities.

There are specially designed classrooms for woodwork, sewing, home economics, computer studies, music studies, art and textile work in addition to general teaching classrooms. Each classroom has a central computer with Internet access monitored by the teacher, with four computer stations for student use. There is also a fully equipped computer room for specialty classes.

Northlands-Nordelta

Nordelta, Argentina

Northlands-Nordelta
Nordelta, Argentina

Criteria
Flexibility / Community

Architect
Jeffrey Berk and Fernando Diez

Type of School
Primary and lower secondary

No. of Students
300

Type of Project
New building

Gross Surface Area
1 800 m2

Year of Completion
2001

Client
Asociación Civil de Beneficencia
Northlands

This school was initially designed in the context of creating a centre for a new town. It provides a community gathering place together with an educational facility that promotes growth and development inside and out.

The cloister

The main feature is a cloister, the structure of the primary school. The cloister includes a colonnade with a wide eve. Another important feature is the secondary school, organised in a long axis opening towards the sport fields.

As the master plan is being completed in stages, each independent building must be able to connect easily to the next. This happens at ground level or through bridges in the first floor. Each independent section of the school is joined to the others with a huge roof that also covers the common patio.

Windows inside and out

Each section is transparent in its interior. Classrooms are divided from the main corridor with furniture and glass showcases that allow the children to display their work and create intimacy, while letting outsiders see in without intruding. Glass is also used to expose the materials used within the structure. These displays highlight the nature, texture and colour of the building materials so that the children can easily recognise them and understand what function they have in the design of the structure.

Susan Magenta, Head of Northlands-Nordelta, explains the advantages. "The feeling of being in close contact with nature is brought about by large windows; with so much glass everywhere the outdoors are brought inside. At the same time, the classrooms are open to the inside, with glass windows forming a good proportion of the walls giving onto the inside corridors. This allows permanent observation of what is going on in each class. Another advantage of this openness is evident when one shows the school to new parents, as this can easily be done without disturbing the classes in progress. The glass throughout, including the offices, responds to the modern concept of people seeing each other and not being closed off. This promotes community spirit and a sense of belonging, both of which are important to the school."

Nuovo Complesso
Scolastico di Monzambano

Monzambano, Italy

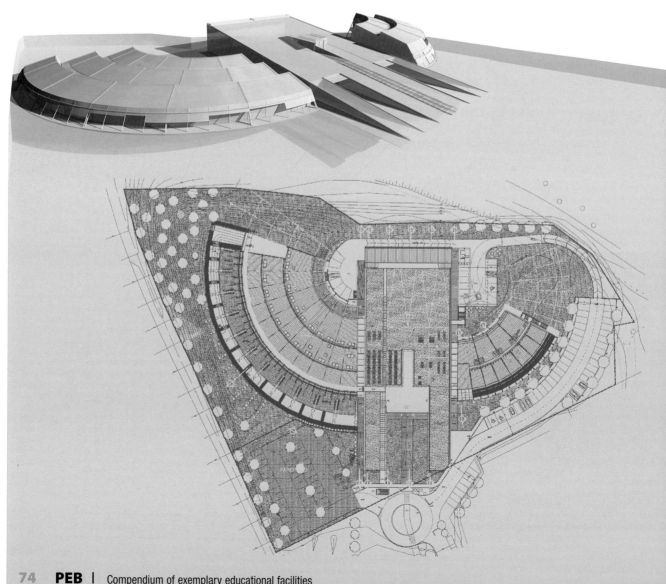

Nuovo Complesso Scolastico di Monzambano
Monzambano, Italy

Criteria
Flexibility / Community / Sustainability

Architect
Ettore Zambelli, Politecnico di Milano
Departimento BEST

Type of School
Primary and lower secondary

No. of Students
650

Type of Project
New building

Gross Surface Area
6 500 m2

Year of Completion
2006

Client
Comune di Monzambano

The new school fits into a delicate environment, close to the Castle of Monzambano, just south of the Lake Garda. To minimise its impact, the main building, containing the auditorium, cafeteria, kitchen and sports hall, is hidden below a green slope (a lawn) that can be used as a park by both students and the public. The two wings containing the classrooms open to the south in order to maximise direct solar gain in the cold periods. Opening clerestories allow for cross ventilation in warm periods, reducing the use of energy-intensive air conditioning.

Inspired design

The new school is designed to minimise its impact both on the existing environment and on natural resources. In this sense, it makes maximum use of natural light and solar radiation to maintain comfortable internal conditions. The teaching areas, especially in the primary school where teaching can be less structured, include a large communal area in the centre of the building, so that different activities can take place, even among students of different classes, in a flexible way.

Other communal areas, stimulating interaction, are the auditorium, canteen and exhibition spaces. These social spaces reflect the sense of community important in the planning of the school itself. The school was designed in close collaboration with the Town of Monzambano and with the teachers and parents involved.

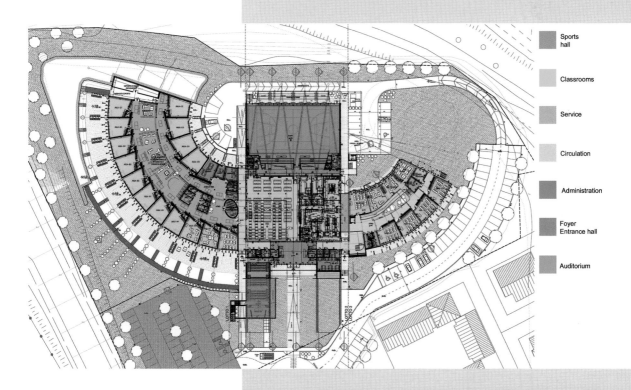

Sports hall

Classrooms

Service

Circulation

Administration

Foyer
Entrance hall

Auditorium

Csapi Általános Iskola, Szakiskola, Diákotthon Kollégium

Csapi, Hungary

The main architectural interest was to adequately mix the old elements of the original building with the substantially new and modern character of this complex.

Csapi Általános Iskola, Szakiskola, Diákotthon Kollégium
Csapi, Hungary

Criteria
Community / Sustainability

Architect
Baratta Éspitész, Mérnök Iroda Kft.

Type of School
Primary, lower secondary and upper special vocational

No. of Students
260

Type of Project
Extension with full scale renovation

Gross Surface Area
1 060 m2

Year of Completion
2005

Client
Ministry of Education

The full scale renovation and extension of this facility for socially disadvantaged students in Hungary has enhanced its important role in the lives of the students and has successfully extended its reach into the local community.

Education and outreach

The principal educational objective for the school is to provide "catching-up" education for socially disadvantaged, mainly Roma students. Many of the students come from distant communities within the region as well as the neighboring settlements, so transportation and resident services are an important aspect of the facility.

The possibility of living in the school's hostel during the week helps develop the social inclusion and education of the students. It offers a unique opportunity for them to study and grow in a positive environment. The students receive the education, supervision, nutrition, social support and vocational training they need to develop and maximise their future options.

An important extension

The local authority and the teaching staff shared their dreams and ideas for a renovation and expansion project with both the Ministry of Education and the project architect. Plans and designs were prepared and implemented on that basis of communication. The main architectural interest was to adequately mix the old elements of the original building with the substantially new and modern character of this complex.

The project employed energy-saving materials and environmentally sensitive applications like solar collectors that provide warm water for the hostel. This has led to expanded environmental education projects within the curriculum.

The new complex has also expanded the school's social function. Neighbouring schools are invited for sports competitions and the annual "Tolerance Days" celebrations. The local community uses the facility for council meetings and wedding ceremonies. Further plans for the institution include a swimming pool and increased international relations with foreign schools.

Viikki Normaalikoulu
Helsinki, Finland

Glass walls in steel frames throughout the structure provide views into the courtyard areas.

Viikki Normaalikoulu
Helsinki, Finland

Criteria
Flexibility / Community

Architect
Markku Erholtz, Ark-house
Arkkitehdit Oy

Type of School
Primary to tertiary

No. of Students
1 000

Type of Project
New building

Gross Surface Area
14 449 m2

Year of Completion
2003

Client
City of Helsinki Department of Education

The Viikki Teacher Training School, located in the center of the Viikki residential area, is a primary to tertiary level school that is used as the training school for the Helsinki University's Department of Teacher Training. It is an impressive work and study facility for 1 200 users.

Corridors, courtyards and common areas

The restrictions of the limited plot area, together with the functional requirements, largely dictated the basic form of the building. The main entrance and the entrance court of the secondary school are at one end of the plot, with the primary school entrance and schoolyard at the other. The two main sections are connected by an internal "main street", along which common social areas such as the restaurant, library, auditoriums and lobbies are located.

The corridors accessing the classrooms and other areas work like secondary streets crossing the main street. Glass walls in steel frames throughout the structure provide views into the courtyard areas. Each section is designed with different materials and finishes for distinct character in each space. The courtyards are also used for teaching purposes.

Teaching plans

A facility for such a large number of users requires not only excellent spatial organisation, but also consultation with all the teacher groups to ensure the facility meets its purpose of providing functional training and learning for everybody.

The school offers state-of-the-art information technology applications, including Internet connections and data projectors in every classroom. Particular attention was given to equipping the auditoriums with exemplary theatre technology.

National University of Singapore High School of Mathematics and Science

Singapore

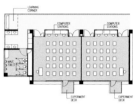

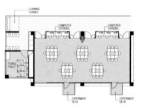

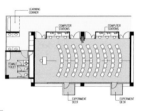

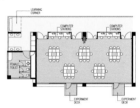

National University of Singapore High School of Mathematics and Science
Singapore

Criteria
Flexibility / Sustainability

Architect
Pit Li Phan, CPG Consultants Pte. Ltd.

Type of School
Lower and upper secondary and tertiary

No. of Students
1 250

Type of Project
New building

Gross Surface Area
39 200 m2

Year of Completion
2005

Client
Ministry of Education

The building is conceived as a three-dimensional tool that forms an active part of learning, and is no longer just a passive container of activities.

The NUS High School is a first-of-its-kind upper secondary school in Singapore developed and managed with a special emphasis on mathematics and science. Its unique educational programme presents an opportunity for the campus to set a new paradigm, to inspire new learning, and to embody the school's beliefs and philosophies of education.

A school to teach and inspire

The design aims to create a stimulating environment that supports project- and enquiry-based learning, where the building is conceived as a three-dimensional tool that forms an active part of learning, and is no longer just a passive container of activities. CPG Consultants have designed the school to be future-enabling by ensuring the facilities are flexible and adaptable and can accommodate future changes in order to remain relevant. The school is also a place where students come together to socialise and form friendships. Various social hubs and gathering spaces have been integrated within the school complex to help foster a sense of community between students.

Flexible future design

The design is driven by the need to meet future requirements. To achieve this, the school needs to be flexible so that it can evolve over time and change easily in response to pedagogical developments. All science laboratories are located on one level linked to the concourse, which is conceived as a "free" space, easily converted to accommodate study benches, learning pods and science exhibitions.

The classrooms are designed in modular pairs. The standard module allows rooms to be inter-convertible, and the pairing allows two rooms to be combined to accommodate different learning modes and settings when the need arises.

NUS High School is an exciting example of new design concepts that transform learning ideas into architecture in order for the building itself to be used as a learning tool.

Gymnase et Centre d'Enseignement Professionnel
Morges, Switzerland

Gymnase et Centre d'Enseignement Professionnel
Morges, Switzerland

Criteria
Sustainability

Architect
Consortium Planification Marcelin, GeninascaDelefortrie SA and Tekhne Management SA

Type of School
Upper secondary and tertiary

No. of Students
800 full-time, 2 000 part-time

Type of Project
New building

Gross Surface Area
11 180 m2

Year of Completion
2003

Client
Canton de Vaud, Département de la Formation et de la Jeunesse

The Morges College and Vocational Training Centre combines two types of institutions on a site that already accommodates one of Switzerland's oldest schools of agriculture. The innovative and sustainable design of the site and its diverse but complementary facilities bring a new balance and synergy to the space.

A compact collage

The project was the result of a competition in which 170 plans were submitted, and makes excellent use of a compact site without disrupting the harmony of the existing environment. Given the magnitude of the educational programme, the project offers a human scale response where each of the three schools has its own identity, yet shares certain facilities in a "dialogue" with the other entities. The site thus offers a form of communal life where each institution can participate in its own way.

Like a collage, the composition, complex as it is, combines various elements in a harmonious and coherent whole. Linked by a semi-underground multi-purpose common area, the new buildings give the site balance with their varied characteristics and use of natural elements.

Ecological principles

Ecological principles were applied throughout the entire project. Important sustainable design applications include roofs planted with vegetation, the recovery of rainwater for sanitary facilities, solar panels for hot water, and the use of wood for surfaces in the playgrounds, classrooms and sports rooms as well as for heating the whole site.

The vast majority of the teachers and pupils appreciate the architecture of the buildings, their modern and uncluttered appearance, and the living areas provided. The combination of two types of schools on the same site represents a profound change in attitudes, seen as a portent of hope for the future. In addition, thanks to its particularly thorough planning and construction, the new complex is well integrated with the previously existing buildings and surrounding landscape.

Blásalir
Reykjavik, Iceland

Blásalir
Reykjavik, Iceland

Criteria
Flexibility / Security

Architect
Manfred Vilhjalmsson and Steinar
Sigurdsson

Type of School
Pre-primary

No. of Students
86 full-time, 4 part-time

Type of Project
New building

Gross Surface Area
4 608 m2

Year of Completion
1999

Client
City of Reykjavik

Design aspects to meet the requirements of users with special needs add to the building's esthetical value and functionality.

The Blásalir preschool is designed to be appealing to the eyes of small children. A bright yellow pyramid rises from the roof, and earth berms surrounding the exterior make the building seem lower than it really is. The door to the main entry is decorated with artwork, and a decorative mirror is located in the foyer. It is a traditional building plan with some noteworthy exceptions.

Inventive play space

A common play area located under the pyramid roof connects homerooms and creates opportunities for social interaction. Large doors separate the homerooms from the play area, which also contains a specialised art workshop. This multipurpose area overlooks and is connected by low gates to a larger, sheltered external patio and playground for multipurpose activities.

The facility serves both children and staff well. The school philosophy places an emphasis on learning by doing and on the use of natural materials such as water, sand, clay and wood. There is an excellent facility for water games, a kiln for clay work and a wood workshop. The area between classrooms is good for role-playing and provides useful floor space for educational games. Playing is the child's way to learn; drawing, painting, modeling and other activities that stimulate creativity are emphasised in the curriculum. The well designed kitchen garden is an important part of the school grounds.

Security, flexibility and responsibility

Student safety and security was an important concern in the building design. All necessary measures are taken as to fire and other hazards, including fire and burglary alarms and escape doors in every room of the building. Other design features add flexibility to the educational environment.

The playground for the youngest children is located near the entrance where wind is minimal. Design aspects to meet the requirements of users with special needs also add to the building's esthetical value and functionality. The collection of recyclable materials, as well as the opportunity to grow plants in the garden, help children develop responsibility and respect for the world around them.

Cowgate Under 5's Centre
Edinburgh, United Kingdom (Scotland)

Collaboration between practitioners and architects – paying particular attention to lighting, colour, the auditory and tactile environment, and the three planes of wall, floor and ceiling – was essential to creating the learning environment in which interaction between the children, staff and parents takes place.

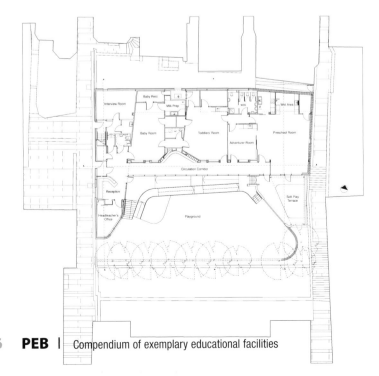

Cowgate Under 5's Centre
Edinburgh, United Kingdom (Scotland)

Criteria
Flexibility / Community / Security

Architect
Allan Murray Architects

Type of School
Pre-primary

No. of Students
57

Type of Project
New building

Gross Surface Area
404 m2

Year of Completion
2002

Client
City of Edinburgh Council, Education Department

The Centre is located in the heart of the Old Town of Edinburgh in a small square flanked by closes that run downhill from the Royal Mile. The clean-cut, crisp design, using glass, metal roofing and a simple rendering contrasts with the surrounding traditional and vernacular environment. The attractive and natural organisation of the school promotes creative and independent learning with flexible open spaces where parents, teachers and students interact.

The children's spaces are located off a circulation/activity area with its attractive, fully glazed wall, leading to a terrace overlooking the tree lined courtyard play area. Accessed by a ramp and steps, the courtyard provides space for informal social interaction and larger organised activities.

Designed to be flexible

There are three inter-connecting classrooms on the ground floor which open up to a glazed hallway, linking internal spaces to an outside garden. The inter-connected spaces allow the children to move freely to other areas. This has also encouraged the children to be more independent; it has helped develop their autonomy as they confidently move from room to room, with freedom to work inside or out. This supports the view that children are capable, resourceful learners.

"Flexible use of space, made possible by the use of moveable partitions and screens, creates options for wide and small spaces for solitude and privacy, supporting change throughout the year, to give creative opportunities to stimulate the imagination and senses and enable children to create their own spaces," says Head Teacher Lynn McNair. The children can create temporary environments autonomously. Mirrors and lighting are used to form spaces within spaces, and other materials are used to define temporary boundaries.

Stimulating the senses

A confident use of light throughout the building adds an emotive component. There are attractive filters of light created by curved windows in all the classrooms. All the classrooms have a glass front, which links them to the hallway and garden. The subtle colours were chosen to allow for "naturalness" within, connecting environments inside and out.

Support and ancillary areas for each age function are located in the sheltering rear of the Centre. The entrance and staff accommodation are located in a two-storey section flanking one of the closes, above the children's spaces. A terrace off the upper floor staff room overlooks the courtyard.

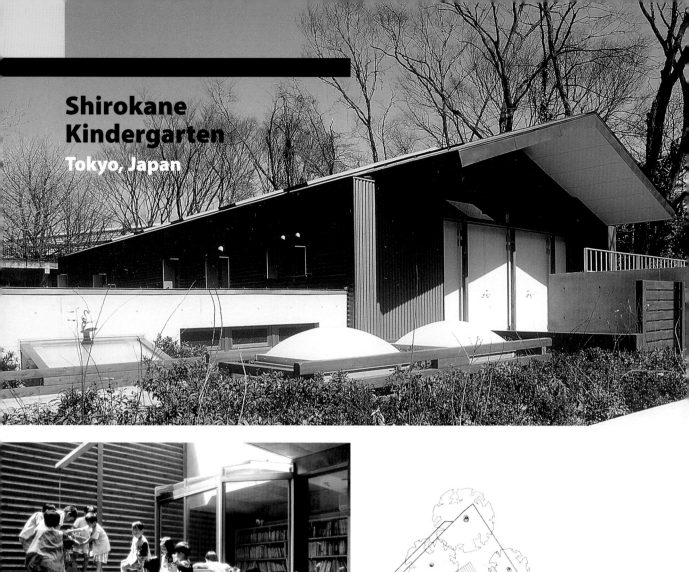

Shirokane Kindergarten
Tokyo, Japan

Shirokane Kindergarten
Tokyo, Japan

Criteria
Flexibility / Community

Architect
Mitsuhiro Suda

Type of School
Pre-primary

No. of Students
165

Type of Project
New building

Gross Surface Area
1 052 m2

Year of Completion
2000

Client
Shirokane Kindergarten

Providing a serene environment for learning and play, this new building for the Shirokane Kindergarten in Tokyo was funded in large part by former students going back as far as 50 years, who fondly remembered their experience at the kindergarten and wanted to contribute to its future. Many parents and graduates were also involved in the design concept with the architecture committee, and this sense of tradition is a major aspect of the new building.

Traditional lessons of life

An important educational aspect of the school is that children learn to respect the traditions and manners of their culture through the art and decorations set on the *Toko-no-ma* (Japanese alcove) in the plaza and a series of ornamental counters. A main design goal was to make this building the vessel of architectural culture, not only for children, but for adults as well.

Various design ideas have been introduced so that children can experience the wonders of seasonal and weather changes, and through the usage of these elements children can stimulate and develop their natural abilities, such as receptivity, imagination and vitality. The rain-fall steps where water flows when it rains are used to foster this curiosity and sensitivity in the young learner. Also, unique forms of built-in furniture, in the corridor or in the half covered plaza, stimulate the children's natural curiosity and allow them to explore and play energetically in a safe, open space.

This new kindergarten building is closely connected with an exterior playground, linked to the half covered plaza at the corner. Children can move back and forth freely between the building, plaza and playground. Even on a rainy day, the students can be active on the wooden lattice in the plaza. During class time, these spaces become a place of serenity, where children learn about tradition and manners through decorations in the alcoves and niches arranged in every corner.

Children can experience the wonders of seasonal and weather changes, and through the art and decorations set on the *Toko-no-ma* (Japanese alcove) in the plaza and a series of ornamental counters.

Groupe Scolaire Martin Peller
Reims, France

Groupe Scolaire Martin Peller
Reims, France

Criteria
Flexibility / Community

Architect
Dominique Coulon

Type of School
Pre-primary and primary

No. of Students
274

Type of Project
New building

Gross Surface Area
5 244 m2

Year of Completion
2004

Client
City of Reims

A bold and modern design concept with bright colours and interesting shapes, the Martin Peller School offers an innovative educational programme within a distinctive structure in a traditional urban setting.

Fully equipped and accessible facilities

The facility includes classrooms, a dormitory, physical education hall, multipurpose room, multimedia room, audio-visual room, reception areas, a staff room, libraries, playgrounds, a refectory and kitchenettes. The physical layout is designed around two levels of education – pre-primary and primary – or *"cycles"*, with some joint nursery/elementary functions. All elementary classrooms are wired for and equipped with computers, and a computer/multimedia room is shared with nursery pupils. The facility is accessible and open to families, pupils and local residents outside school hours. All facilities are accessible to people with reduced mobility.

Functional planning and a programme that reflects key goals

The programme and building design were based on new programme guidelines for levels of education, new teaching practices, and the facilities required for learning and physical/sporting/cultural activities. These guidelines led to the project's key features, namely:

- The layout of classrooms, storage units and water supply, with adjacent handicraft/cultural rooms for joint activities.
- Motor skills and sports/physical activities with a large, flexible space for sports, music and movement activities (shared by elementary and nursery pupils), and a physical education room.
- ICT wiring and equipment throughout the school.
- Shared-use areas available to both the elementary and nursery schools, such as a dedicated eating space.
- Teachers working in teams.
- Areas to meet the demand for outdoor space, in particular for gardening activities and of course playgrounds with the necessary play facilities.

Harmony Primary School
Perth, Australia

Harmony Primary School
Perth, Australia

Criteria
Flexibility / Community / Sustainability

Architect
Taylor Robinson Architects

Type of School
Pre-primary and primary

No. of Students
330

Type of Project
New building

Gross Surface Area
4 414 m2

Year of Completion
2004

Client
Department of Education and Training

D esigned to incorporate Ecologically Sustainable Design (ESD) initiatives, Harmony Primary School integrates these principles into everyday school life. It is a definitive example of sustainable design and construction with significant environmental and educational outcomes.

The forms and materials used reflect the unique nature of the school, and have been developed to enhance ESD educational benefits. The roof shapes, generated to allow for natural ventilation and to capture daylight, are internally expressed with raked ceilings, and provide exciting spaces for learning. The planning maximises the use of external areas by the school community and minimises the use of resources, while the orientation of the buildings makes full benefit of passive thermal design.

Enhancing the learning environment

Water efficiency is achieved through the collection of stormwater, re-use of greywater and careful design of landscaping. Energy efficiency is achieved through the use of daylighting, natural ventilation and passive thermal design, reducing the need for resources. These elements also increase the indoor air quality and add to the learning environment, improving student performance. A building management system is used to enhance students' understanding of their impact on the environment.

The use of visible elements increases the educational opportunities and includes rainwater tanks, solar powered lights, charcoal coloured thermal walls, louvres and renewable materials, such as plantation timber for the roof structure and Marmoleum® floor coverings.

The school community have embraced the environmental opportunities offered by the design of the school, and have increased their awareness of their built and natural environment. Activities such as composting and recycling waste, re-using and recycling paper, and investigating alternatives sources for fertiliser have been incorporated into lessons. Sensory gardens, permaculture gardens and a recycling area have been incorporated into the design for school and community use.

Community outreach

The co-location of the community centre on the primary school site allows for the involvement of the local residents. Events such as a Sustainability Extravaganza have been held to educate the community about sustainable living and demonstrate the school's ESD initiatives.

The school is also involved in managing an adjacent ecological park. This has a direct link to the water and resource management initiatives displayed within the school.

De Levensboom
Kortrijk-Marke, Belgium

De Levensboom
Kortrijk-Marke, Belgium

Criteria
Flexibility / Community

Architect
Isabelle Jacques and Bernard Wittevrongel

Type of School
Primary

No. of Students
160

Type of Project
New building

Gross Surface Area
1 800 m2

Year of Completion
1999

Client
VZW De Levensboom

This sustainable school project qualifies the different areas of the building site and allows for maximum flexibility in the use of common grounds. The school buildings have been simplified to a minimal and clearly identifiable plan. Central is the forum, a major meeting space for the parents, children and their teachers, framed by classrooms on two sides, enclosed by the common facilities on the third side, and open to the natural spaces.

De Levensboom – TheTree of Life

The school building creates the necessary environment to organise the pedagogical programme inspired by the co-operative Freinet practice. From a wooden terrace, one gains access through the common facilities to the forum. Basically a playground, the forum favours daily exchanges between parents, children and teachers, the key of Freinet pedagogy.

Circulation between the different classrooms and the common building is organised outside under a covered walkway, lifted from the natural level, animating the central space. The topography favours direct contact with the outside and includes an adventure garden, a small natural reserve with vegetable gardens grown by the classes.

Linked to the forum, classrooms expand outdoors easily. This use of space reinforces the sense of community and connections between classes, stressing co-operation. Classes are not focused on the blackboard, but rather on the multiple activity areas.

The children make the most of the different opportunities of the site, inside as well as outside the building. The flexibility of the classrooms lets them enjoy the different activities in their own environment. The diversity of exterior spaces, the organised playground, the wild reservation and the small gardens provide opportunities to express their imagination and to understand nature and how society works.

Basic materials – parent participation

The restricted budget demanded simple, standardised elements, including the façade panels and window frames. The different access spaces are identified by masonry, whereas other parts have an open wooden cladding. The roof, with its wooden structure and natural aluminum covering, unifies the whole project.

Thanks to the openness of the entrance hall, administration and teachers' facilities, parents feel welcomed and take part in the school activities. Parents also take an active role in the pedagogical and financial aspects, expressed in the polyvalent room and the theatre.

École du Petit-Lancy
Lancy/Geneva, Switzerland

The Petit-Lancy School successfully combines elements to create new areas and aspects of primary school teaching.

École du Petit-Lancy
Lancy/Geneva, Switzerland

Criteria
Flexibility

Architect
CLR Chevalley Longchamp Russbach
Architectes fas sia

Type of School
Primary

No. of Students
350

Type of Project
New building

Gross Surface Area
4 180 m2

Year of Completion
2004

Client
Ville de Lancy

Incorporating the most recent concepts of flexible design for schools and classrooms alongside traditional teaching and learning methods, the Petit-Lancy School successfully combines these elements to create new areas and aspects of primary school teaching. The school includes 14 classrooms with rooms for creative workshops and other extracurricular activities such as games and dancing. These teaching areas are grouped together in an open, flexible plan that maximises the available space and inspires creative teaching and learning.

Adaptable teaching areas

In order to provide teachers with a degree of flexibility in the use of their classrooms, the concept of "decompartmentalisation" has been utilised in the school design. Decompartmentalisation refers here to grouping pupils around an activity for a given time. The number of pupils grouped together can vary, and groups can include pupils from different classes.

The system is conceived as an additional option to the conventional use of classrooms operating separately. A set of sliding doors allows classes to be grouped according to the activities of the moment. Groups can be formed by isolating them from the rest of the building in order to work together on a particular subject.

For example, if two neighbouring classes want to get together on the subject of astronomy three half days a week for a month, they are isolated from the rest of the building by closing the red doors in the corridor, and creating a common space by opening the sliding partitions of their own classrooms. The corridor is then appropriated and provides an additional working area while linking the classes in the same group. Each decompartmentalised area has its own washrooms and staircase, thus making each group independent.

Recent developments and future benefits

To avoid moving the classroom furniture in order to use the corridor, the cloakroom benches can serve as seats, and classroom desk tops (which are easily detachable) are used as tables. It is thus possible to work in groups for a few hours and then close the sliding doors of the classrooms to work separately for the rest of the day. The red doors in the corridor can also serve to separate elementary and primary areas, and they can act as fire doors if necessary. The generous width of the doors between the classrooms and the corridor provide a wide sightline, allowing good supervision by teachers.

The plan was implemented following an architecture competition for which the jury was composed mainly of representatives of the future users. The decompartmentalisation was requested by the Department of Public Education taking into account recent developments in education and trends in primary school teaching.

Geumho Elementary School
Seoul, Korea

Geumho Elementary School
Seoul, Korea

Criteria
Flexibility / Community / Finance

Architect
Garam Architects & Associates

Type of School
Primary

No. of Students
1 886

Type of Project
New building

Gross Surface Area
14 105 m2

Year of Completion
2001

Client
Seongdong-gu District Office of Education

This public elementary school represents a poignant triumph within the cultural and educational climate of the community. It also presents a unique example of new funding strategies for public schools in Korea. The successful co-operation and collaboration in raising capital to build and develop the facility has resulted in a significant addition to Seoul's educational and cultural aspect.

Shaping the space

The basic form of the structure is composed of various dramatic shapes. A square, a semi cylinder and a circular cone define the main buildings, while the visual experience of the interior is enveloping and rich. The attractive façade also reflects the essential idea of the educational and architectural interests of the school.

The multi-functional space plan allows for various teaching-learning methods within a new national educational curriculum. The areas dedicated to common use such as the swimming pool, sports centre, library, auditorium and playground are all important spaces with large open designs. These areas were of particular interest for this school conceived and developed for community use.

Financed for public use

Geumho Elementary School was built using an alternative way of financing the capital expenditure. Under the most common practice in Korea, the public schools have been financed and operated through the national budget. This school is unique in that the local public bodies provided the funding and the local community took part in the planning and design of the facility. It therefore integrates the teaching-learning space for students with facilities for the community, including space for cultural activities, continuing education programmes and underground parking for this high-density area.

The total building cost for the project was financed by the national Ministry of Education, the Seoungdong-gu District Office of Education and the Seoul municipal government. This collaboration, together with the involvement of the local community in the planning and design of the facility, has resulted in a nationally recognised building with a successful community-school partnership.

Griffeen Valley Educate Together School
Lucan, Co. Dublin, Ireland

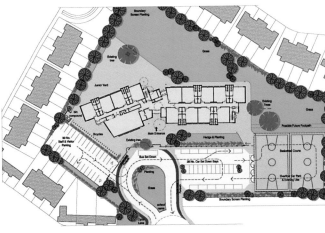

Griffeen Valley Educate Together School
Lucan, Co. Dublin, Ireland

Criteria
Flexibility / Sustainability / Finance

Architect
Coady Partnership Architects

Type of School
Primary

No. of Students
215 (capacity 480)

Type of Project
New building

Gross Surface Area
2 171 m2

Year of Completion
2004

Client
Department of Education and Science

The successful growth of the Irish economy over recent years, resulting in an explosion of housing developments and rapid expansion of cities and towns, has created pressures on educational infrastructure. In response, the Department of Education and Science sought to procure as a test case a new primary school on a fast track programme that would set exemplary standards for future primary school accommodation. From submission of tender through the statutory planning process to completion on site, the development and construction of Griffeen Valley's new school took just nine months.

Sustainability and scale

The building has been designed for long life and durability. Sustainability, ease of maintenance and cost-in-use have all been factored into the design. The timber frame has allowed high levels of insulation to be used and facilitated off-site manufacture whilst on-site work proceeded. A light, steel frame integrated within the timber frame supports a pre-cast concrete first floor slab. The building is part single and part two storey with a cranked linear plan that provides scale and prominence to the building as seen on arrival, with the assembly hall forming a special feature on the western end.

Bright design for development

The school provides a rich and flexible environment to fully support the social, academic and physical development of the pupils. The "Educate Together" ethos means that the new school has pupils of different cultural backgrounds and varying abilities. Particular means were incorporated to provide improved and easy access for a wider range of physical disabilities as well. The use of voids, vibrant colours and high ceilings animate the teaching spaces, and recesses for seating and displays in the corridors add further dimensions to the design.

Principal Tomas O'Dulaing praises the foresight of the design team. "Ours is an 'Educate Together' school. It prides itself on its openness and warmth, and it was very important to school staff and management that these aspects would be reflected in the design and layout. We feel strongly that this has been achieved. Even on the darkest days the school rooms and corridors are as bright as they could be. On sunny days the clever, premeditated design allows every possible stream of light to weave its magic in this lovely building."

Ikeda Elementary School
Osaka Prefecture, Japan

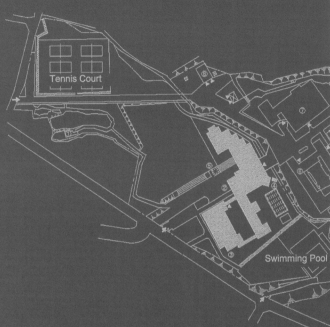

Tennis Court

Swimming Pool

Ikeda Elementary School
Osaka Prefecture, Japan

Criteria
Flexibility / Security

Architect
Kyodo Sekkei

Type of School
Primary

No. of Students
693

Type of Project
New building, extension

Gross Surface Area
9 202 m2

Year of Completion
2004

Client
Osaka Kyoiku University

In June, 2001, Ikeda Elementary School experienced a horrible attack by an intruder. The survivors of this terrible incident can be proud of their courageous response. The whole community has come together to create a safe, strong and inspired school building – an international model for school security.

Enhanced surveillance

Under the motto of "protecting our children through surveillance", the school buildings feature copious use of transparent glass to increase visibility. That means the teachers and staff can easily watch the children on the playground and in the classrooms, in addition to seeing anyone who visits the school. This creates a safe and secure environment that enables the children to better concentrate on their studies.

The main gates of the elementary school and of the attached Ikeda Middle and High Schools have been limited to one location where crime-prevention devices have been installed, including an interphone with a camera and an infrared sensor. When the electric lock on the main gate is released, a signal is activated in the faculty room and office.

Cameras have been installed to survey areas on the school grounds that cannot be seen from the administrative areas. To ensure that the gymnasium hall did not impede the view to the outside, its outer walls are glass.

New buildings are planned to further enclose the campus and provide new and modern facilities for the students.

Security and unity

The administration section is centrally located in order to have a vast view of the site from the inside. Ordinary classrooms are located in the west wing, and special classrooms in the east wing. The west wing has an open form in order to adapt to various classroom configurations. A faculty area has been located in one corner of the workspace to create a feeling of security and unity as faculty members are always nearby.

The terrible incident of 2001 affected every member of the Ikeda community and touched school communities everywhere. The efforts of education officials, architects, the school administration, teachers, staff and especially the group of parents most affected by the incident has led to an outstanding school and a safe environment where children can study, learn and grow without fear.

Kingsmead Primary School
Kingsmead, United Kingdom (England)

Kingsmead Primary School
Kingsmead, United Kingdom (England)

Criteria
Flexibility / Sustainability / Security

Architect
Craig White, White Design Associates Ltd.

Type of School
Primary

No. of Students
199

Type of Project
New building

Gross Surface Area
1 310 m2

Year of Completion
2004

Client
Cheshire County Council

The design intention behind the proposal for Kingsmead Primary School was to deliver an exemplary school of sustainable design and construction. The school integrates many of the principles enshrined in the Department for Education and Skills' (DfES) "Schools for the Future" agenda and demonstrates its three main principles: 1. To raise educational standards. 2. To produce inspiring, flexible exemplary designs. 3. To deliver schools to a high standard, rapidly, cost-effectively and consistently.

This ethos informs every aspect of the design, from its orientation on the site, to the selection of natural materials, the use of natural ventilation, daylighting techniques and the landscape concept. The design took best practice guidance from DfES as a starting point, and sought to go beyond them. The procurement options for the building also helped to achieve the environmental targets by sourcing local materials and labour where possible.

Energy efficiency measures and renewable energy technologies

The proposal innovates in the organisation of space in a number of ways. The north facing classroom design ensures classrooms receive consistent and high light levels. The project uses natural ventilation techniques to minimise the use of mechanical ventilation. Careful integration of the Building Management System allows each space to be ventilated automatically while maintaining acoustic separation.

The school was designed to be energy efficient by natural daylighting to reduce the reliance on electric lights and super insulation to reduce heating costs. Further measures such as rainwater collections and waste minimisation have been put in place. The school utilises three forms of renewable energy: photovoltaics, solar water heating and biomass.

Safety, security and steps for the future

The scheme incorporated provision of secure boundary fencing, automatic fire detection (linked back to a monitoring station) and a sophisticated closed circuit television system (also linked to a monitoring station) that can be used as an educational resource during the day and a security measure during evenings and weekends.

The next steps for Kingsmead include expanding the monitoring system to better measure the energy used in the building. This data will be saved onto a computer and used as a teaching and learning aid. Monitoring the energy use so closely also will enable the most energy efficient use of the building. Other important objectives are to achieve a surplus of energy generated by the solar photovoltaic system for export to the national grid, and to change the fuel for the biomass boiler from wood pellets to locally sourced woodchip.

Mawson Lakes School
Adelaide, Australia

Mawson Lakes School
Adelaide, Australia

Criteria
Flexibility / Community / Sustainability

Architect
MGT Canberra Architects and Russell & Yelland Architects

Type of School
Primary

No. of Students
340

Type of Project
New building

Gross Surface Area
2 144 m2

Year of Completion
2003

Client
Department of Education and Children's Services

Mawson Lakes School is located on a narrow site between the Mawson Lakes town centre and Dry Creek reserve. The school provides a sensitive and stimulating educational environment with thoughtful orientation and sustainable design using modern, large volume learning areas that allow in natural light and provide views to the outdoor areas.

Unique windows to the world

The school plan comprises four main single-storey flexible learning spaces accessible from a covered spine to the west and abutting the eastern street boundary. The courtyards opening off the main areas provide an extension of the learning space, and the doors can be fully opened for free access between indoors and out. The varying bays and windows, offering visual interest and engagement for pedestrians, are primarily places of retreat and small groupings for students within, and provide unique windows to the world for outlook and display. Also, windows into the wall construction of masonry, timber and insulation enable further teaching opportunites on environmental design.

Environmental design

Solar and thermal ventilation chimneys, large roof overhangs, sun shaded windows, solar water heating and water recycling are just some of the devices which express the priority for sensitive environmental design in the project. The Building Management System is accessible from classroom laptops with wireless technology, and a green house and planting beds in classroom courtyards further reflect the school's commitment to a holistic learning environment.

Community connections

The Dry Creek reserve, the town centre and the university are also utilised as learning resources. The administration and shared community/school library are located in the Mawson Centre, the community hub 500 metres from the school, giving a focus to all the educational services available to the area.

Over 40 different community and educational groups were consulted prior to commencement of the design. The students were involved from the very beginning of the project right through to the end of construction, and designed the major screen wall artwork in collaboration with local artist Leslie Matthews. All the parties involved have learned a great deal together as they have explored the relationship between learning and its environment in the new century.

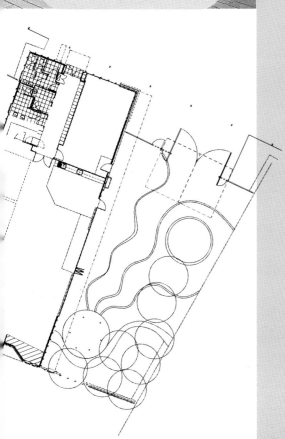

Nesting Primary School
Skellister, South Nesting, United Kingdom (Scotland)

CLASSROOM 1

STORE 7

STORE 8

ART/MUSIC ROOM

STORE 'R'

CLASSROOM 2

QUIET WORK AREA

STAFF ROOM

LIBRARY/ RESOURCE AREA

W.C.

DISABLED USERS TOILET

HEAD TEACHERS OFFICE

SECRETARYS OFFICE

CLEANERS STORE

BOYS TOILETS

STORE

STORE 5

CLOAKROOM

ENTRANCE

GIRLS TOILETS

STORE 3

STORE 4

STORE 1

STORE 2

PLANT ROOM

GAMES HALL

KITCHEN

Nesting Primary School
Skellister, South Nesting,
United Kingdom (Scotland)

Criteria
Flexibility / Community / Sustainability

Architect
Barbara Dinnage

Type of School
Primary

No. of Students
26

Type of Project
New building

Gross Surface Area
630 m2

Year of Completion
2004

Client
Shetland Islands Council Community Services

The guiding vision for the construction of the Nesting Primary School was to provide a contemporary educational facility, economic to run and maintain, that responds to the needs and interests of each building user, while connecting the school with the surrounding community and landscape. The simple, flexible and efficient design incorporates important concepts of sustainability into its construction, offers a bright and stimulating environment for learning, and maintains the option for future expansion. The school also demonstrates innovative solutions with regards to full access for all users and passive energy conservation measures. The use of local materials integrate its design into the landscape.

Main design concepts and strategies include:

- Orientation of classrooms for light, warmth and views across the landscape.
- Acoustic ceilings which give an immediate calming effect.
- Appropriate use of bright colours, and pupil and teacher involvement in this choice.
- Windows which open to provide natural ventilation, with internal blinds to stop overheating.
- Careful detailing to keep floor levels inside the building the same as ground levels outside, and so dispense with the need for any ramps or handrails.
- Inter-active whiteboards to replace blackboards.
- Maximum use of recycled materials in the construction and materials which can themselves be recycled.
- Bicycle sheds to encourage children to take exercise.
- The acquisition of a large site around the building for future expansion and for the addition of a nursery should the need arise.

An important aspect of the school building is its respect for the surrounding landscape and local community. A main objective was to not only use materials with minimal environmental impact, but to also ensure the use of local materials, traditions and skills in construction. This project uses local stone, Scottish hardwoods and a high quality finish provided by local craftsmen. Colours were chosen in collaboration with end users to harmonise with the countryside. The dark grey, dark blue and orange are colours found in the surrounding mossy and heathery hills. The school continues to attract attention from near and far, and environmentalists are currently planning native woodlands on the site.

North Kildare Educate Together School
Celbridge, Co. Kildare, Ireland

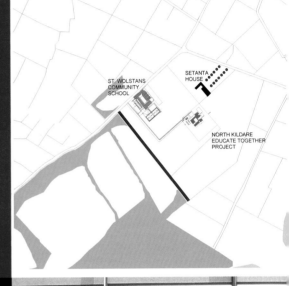

ST. WOLSTANS COMMUNITY SCHOOL

SETANTA HOUSE

NORTH KILDARE EDUCATE TOGETHER PROJECT

North Kildare Educate Together School
Celbridge, Co. Kildare, Ireland

Criteria
Flexibility

Architect
Grafton Architects

Type of School
Primary

No. of Students
250

Type of Project
New building

Gross Surface Area
1 750 m2

Year of Completion
2003

Client
Department of Education and Science

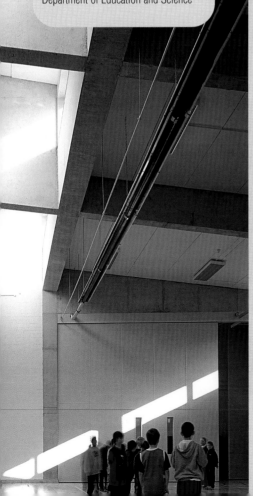

North Kildare Educate Together School is the first custom-built, integrated primary school in Ireland. It has ten classrooms, including two specialised teaching classrooms for children with autism.

The plan rotates around a central main courtyard, the classrooms acting as independent satellites, each a "studio" with its own intimate den and enclosed garden court. Brick walls, plinths and terracotta window sills are used to offer tactility and richness of colour and to define the significant public spaces within the building, such as the general purpose hall, library and garden.

The Department of Education and Science requires that schools are single storey, where possible, and are constructed in exposed concrete block work. Within these constraints, together within the strict cost limits, the architects liberated the design with a pre-cast concrete roof. The copper clad, wave-like roof, with light chimneys to each classroom, brings a spatial complexity and sense of weight to the building. A large roof light capturing the south sun opens and animates the general purpose room, which is positioned close to the main entrance and is the largest space in the school.

Principal Rita Galvin explains the "studio" classroom layout. "One of the most remarkable features of the building is the wonderful light filled classrooms and corridors throughout. Each room has its own den area, a space loved by children and teachers alike. It is a class or individual story area, stage area, project work area or simply a 'time-out' zone. The circulation spaces overlook a central courtyard garden, and the theme of 'bringing the outdoors in' continues into classrooms where each class enjoys its own individual garden."

Specific design for special needs

A seamless transition from the general school to the specialist classrooms for the children with autism was the central concern of those involved with this project. Specialists, working closely with parents, teachers, the school body and the Department of Education and Science, addressed particular and detailed requirements, which were incorporated in a way to integrate children with autism into the overall school complex.

Principal Galvin sums up the ground-breaking programme. "A central part of the building design has been the integration of the country's first purpose built unit for children with autism. This required research into the very specific needs of these children and once again a child-centred approach was taken by the architects. This unit is now a prototype for future units in the country. Our school community is very proud of our unique building. The staff feels privileged to work with the children in an educational space so appropriately designed to meet all our needs."

Oteha Valley School
North Shore, New Zealand

FRONT ELEVATION

REAR ELEVATION

Oteha Valley School
North Shore, New Zealand

Criteria
Flexibility / Community / Sustainability

Architect
Babbage Consultants Ltd.

Type of School
Primary

No. of Students
185 (capacity 520)

Type of Project
New building

Gross Surface Area
2 233 m2

Year of Completion
2004

Client
Ministry of Education

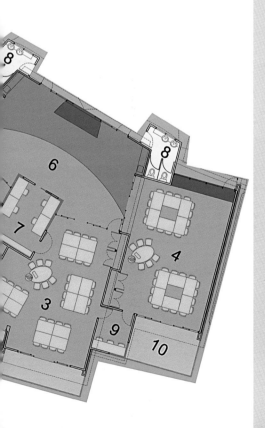

O teha Valley is committed to quality teaching for diverse students, implementing pedagogy well-founded in research that New Zealand educators see as the way of the future. This new school was designed for the characteristics of this approach, its emphasis on success for every student and the expectation that teachers will simultaneously manage the learning for groups of diverse students.

A group vision into design

A group of teaching and learning experts from North Shore City, including a principal, teachers, parents and the architects, devised the vision for this school. They foresaw independent learning within large and small supervised groups in flexible classrooms, commons and exterior spaces. The group created the vision of a school based on an inquiry model in which pupils researched knowledge, brainstormed, set key questions, formed hypotheses, reported their findings and planned consequential actions. The design brief included the flexible spaces, research facilities and Internet access for this approach to teaching and learning.

Creative, flexible pods

This vision led to the essential design idea and the significant architectural interest of Oteha Valley School: detached but identical teaching and learning "pods", designed for maximum flexibility of use.

No classroom has a "teacher-at-the-front" configuration, but each has two glazed walls with large sliding doors, eight data outlets and computers, wireless access to the Internet, exterior decks and access to shared *awhina*, a supervised common space which can be used for art, dance, drama and other group activities.

Each pod has a centrally placed work area for teachers from which they can see all students at all times, and a multi-channel sound field in each classroom and *awhina* which enables teachers' voices to be heard wherever the pupils are working. At the heart of the school is the media centre with the library, conference room and computers for research.

Principal Megan Bowden is excited by the success of the school's design, and by the way pupils and teachers have adapted their practices to make full use of it. "The school buildings place no constraints on what teachers and pupils want to achieve. I can see everything happening and they can see me. I see pupil-centred, pupil-managed learning going on in every pod. We are enabling our students to learn how to learn, to develop lifelong learning skills, and the results to date are so good that we wouldn't change any part of our school or its philosophy. Our school community is very young (this was all farmland just five years ago) and they helped design both our approach to teaching and learning and the shape of the school. They are supportive and proud of both."

Te Matauranga School

Auckland, New Zealand

Te Matauranga School
Auckland, New Zealand

Criteria
Flexibility / Community / Security

Architect
DA Ltd.

Type of School
Primary

No. of Students
450

Type of Project
New building

Gross Surface Area
3 637 m2

Year of Completion
2005

Client
Ministry of Education

The community around Te Matauranga has a rich ethnic diversity with Maori, Samoan, Indian, Tongan and Fijian children making up 90% of the roll. This diversity presents both opportunities for learning and challenges for the new school because of the relatively low socio-economic status of the area. The community wanted a safe and accessible school environment with a strong emphasis on learning. A school built not just for teaching but for children's learning, safety and security as well.

Design responses

Three main concepts were incorporated into the building to address the stated needs of the school community:

- A "street" from which parents could see their children at any time in any space, without disrupting their learning, and in which they could socialise.
- Spaces for specific needs such as reading recovery, speech therapy, social work and a resource teacher, as well as classrooms for teaching and learning in the Maori and Samoan languages. All these facilities assist children to succeed, whatever their needs, in a mainstream educational environment.
- Outdoor play areas safely located so that children cannot be seen from the surrounding roads.

The internal street is the key point of architectural interest and also embodies the design's essential idea: a calm, safe, accessible and well-equipped school strongly linked to its community.

Learning how to learn

Extensive pre-design community consultation identified the community's desire for high academic expectations and an emphasis on learning how to learn. The focal point of the street is the information centre where key literacy, inquiry learning and information technology skills are enhanced. The street design also included sufficient wireless "airports" for all children to have easy computer access. From age five, the children are taught how to ask questions, access information that is probably not available to them in their homes and follow learning pathways.

The principal of Te Matauranga, Jane Wallis, says the new school is "absolutely and totally effective" and that the architecture strongly supports the school philosophy that focuses on student achievement and partnership with parents. "Everybody in the school can see learning happening, can see the community involvement with dozens of parents in the street and can see special needs being met. It's all about learning in a safe and inclusive environment with lots of technology so that the children can access as much information as children anywhere. We have no barriers to learning here. After one year in these buildings we wouldn't change anything."

Tajimi Junior High School
Gifu-ken, Japan

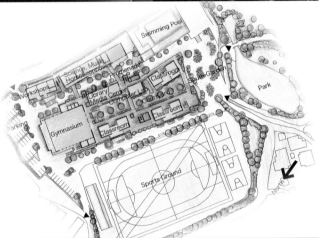

In ordinary schools there are hallways and walls next to classrooms but in our school, a big zelkova tree, the symbol of our school, stands in the courtyard as we step out of our room.

Tajimi Junior High School
Gifu-ken, Japan

Criteria
Flexibility / Community / Sustainability

Architect
Atelier Zo

Type of School
Lower secondary

No. of Students
584

Type of Project
New building

Gross Surface Area
10 546 m2

Year of Completion
2001

Client
Tajimi City

To create a rich educational experience for the lower secondary school students, four themes were established and executed in the development and building of this school, with a focus on integrating natural elements.

Being green

The first theme addresses the importance of living with nature. The site and buildings are covered with plants that blend in with the surrounding hills and park greenery. There are many elements here that enable students to experience the changes of the day and the seasons, and the design utilises important environmental and naturally sensitive applications suitable as educational tools as well. Photovoltaic generation panels set on the roof of the gym can provide 40 kwh of natural electric power. Rainwater is saved, circulated to the ponds on each floor and used for watering the plants. Finally, greening on the rooftop works as a heat-insulating layer, and with the greenery of the courtyard and promenade, adds to the natural landscape.

Developing space

The idea behind the second and third themes is a school as an active living place where people feel they have a place for themselves. All around the facility, there are benches, small corners, and open spaces for people to sit and relax. Each of these places will be someone's favourite and add to their sense of spiritual and physical freedom. Inside and outside, there is a continuity of space that appeals to all five senses. The many exterior stairs connect the courtyard and the rooftop. People circulate freely from inside to outside, up and down, in inspiring open spaces.

Flexibility of use

The objective of the fourth theme is to create a flexible school that can adapt to changing aims and situations day to day. One of the requests from the community was a "school open to the public". The construction of this new school, which was a big project for the local community, needed to involve the community and meet their expectations. The gymnasium and specialised rooms are open to community use, and the space between the school buildings, where local residents can pass, was developed as part of the city park.

Ardscoil Mhuire
Ballinasloe, Co. Galway, Ireland

Ardscoil Mhuire
Ballinasloe, Co. Galway,
Ireland

Criteria
Flexibility

Architect
Grafton Architects

Type of School
Lower and upper secondary

No. of Students
500

Type of Project
New building

Gross Surface Area
4 196 m2

Year of Completion
2003

Client
The Sisters of Mercy, Western Province

"Ardscoil Mhuire is built on a hillside and Grafton Architects have sensitively designed the building, so that it nestles naturally into its surroundings. Despite its size, it lies unobtrusively in the embrace of the rolling landscape," says Principal Mary Malloy, introducing this facility, where the physical reminders of the past are woven into the everyday experience. The school acts as a type of hill town where each student experiences the original geological hillside by means of two gently sloping corridors, which connect the three levels of the school.

The main entrance is protected from the prevailing southwest winds by providing a sequence of ramped spaces that lead up into the sheltered front door. The physical education hall is positioned beside a group of mature native trees, which form a protected entrance route into the hall for independent use by the community.

Courtyards

Each classroom is a separate world. The architectural challenge was to organise the range of rooms, so that the circulation has meaning and the school has a centre. To enrich the educational and architectural character of the school, the general purpose area, library, reception and courtyard have been placed at the centre. Students circulate through these spaces to access either the main courtyard or the three other courtyards, each of which has its own distinct character: the Meditation Court, the Art Court and the Music Court.

In this way, the complex jigsaw of classrooms and other facilities are organised into a coherent and legible place which has a heart, and where each student feels part of an educational community.

Open possibilities

The school's floor plate is pushed into the hill, allowing the roofscape to run parallel with the slope and to form renewed contours lines. The construction method is precise and rational; the resultant volumes formed by the roof – with light boxes and ventilating chimneys – modify and animate the rigorous and economic plan. The internal environment created is full of light with cross ventilation for each classroom. Windows were placed to frame ground views and sky views. Transparency across the plan connects the community of the buildings to each other.

Coláiste Eoin agus Coláiste Íosagáin
Baile An Bhóthair,
Co. Átha Cliath, Ireland

Coláiste Eoin agus Coláiste Íosagáin
Baile An Bhóthair,
Co. Átha Cliath, Ireland

Criteria
Flexibility / Community / Sustainability

Architect
Grafton Architects

Type of School
Lower and upper secondary

No. of Students
900

Type of Project
Extension

Gross Surface Area
3 504 m2

Year of Completion
2003

Client
The Boards of Management of Coláiste
Eoin and Coláiste Íosagáin

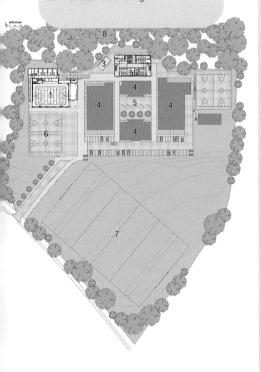

Coláiste Eoin and Coláiste Íosagáin consist of two independent, Irish-speaking schools, one for boys, one for girls, sharing the same site. The original single-storey school buildings form a courtyard, and there is a gaelic football pitch to the south. Within this restricted space, a new four-storey academic building and a new sports hall were constructed for shared use by the two schools. This joint project and the creative collaboration between the Department of Education and Science, parents, students and, of course, the architects have effectively pushed out educational boundaries, anticipating future needs.

In the academic building, vertical cuts were made to allow light into the central, organising corridor and to frame views of the mountains to the south. The sports hall, also used for concerts and other performances, has a curved timber-clad ceiling and wood paneling on the walls, which combine to produce a visually attractive space that enhances the acoustics.

Having found a way of placing the new accommodations on the site, wedged between tall, mature trees to the north and the original buildings to the south, the task was then to stitch together the new and the old, the big and the small. A series of elements were crucial in this process:

- The south-facing surface of the sports hall, with its long seat, acts a backdrop to the play area it addresses.
- A timber canopy, projecting from the sports hall, acts as a sun shade for both the long seat and the interior of the hall.
- A low, concrete and timber-screened pavilion contains the dining and assembly room, its overshooting roof providing an entrance porch to the sports hall and its scale addressing the original school buildings.
- New paths connect the original courtyard to the two new buildings, and ramps connect the lower changing areas at the back of the sports hall to the outdoor play areas.
- Interstitial spaces between the mature trees and new buildings form loose, but legible, outdoor spaces.

Another pivotal element is the new handball alley, dropped casually in the interstitial space between trees and buildings. This is probably the only new outdoor handball alley built in Ireland in the last 50 years. It was important to make a modern space for such an ancient game, enjoyed by students and teachers alike.

Morgan Academy
Dundee, United Kingdom (Scotland)

Morgan Academy
Dundee, United Kingdom (Scotland)

Criteria
Flexibility / Community / Sustainability / Finance

Architect
Dundee City Council, Architectural Services

Type of School
Lower and upper secondary

No. of Students
893

Type of Project
Renovation

Gross Surface Area
7 870 m2

Year of Completion
2004

Client
Dundee City Council, Education Department

S taff, pupils, parents and members of the wider community have individually and collectively praised the reinstatement of Morgan Academy, which is again a centrepiece in the northern inner-city area of Dundee.

The Morgan Academy restoration involved a complex design to rigid standards, dictated by Historic Scotland, to ensure that the Grade A listed building classification was maintained. This baronial style architecture has been preserved as part of Scotland's architectural heritage. The building incorporates the historic architecture of the façade while developing a modern teaching facility within the footprint of the original building. The project demonstrates that historical architecture and new designs can be integrated to provide a functional teaching facility in a modern environment.

Key architectural features, including the tower and spiral staircase, have been maintained and utilised for special education classes. The bulk of the interior space, however, has been transformed into a bright, modern teaching facility designed to meet the new technological age in learning and teaching. All rooms are equipped with network connections and overhead interactive LCD projectors. The large hall and social area provide a focus and meeting area for the school, enhancing the ethos and sense of belonging for the pupils.

This project was implemented through a partnership agreement between client, contractor, consultants, and associated sub-contractors and sub-consultants. The design process was ongoing when the client representatives, which included the headmaster, teaching staff and pupils, joined the project team. All these groups contributed to the design process and ensured that the building was fit for purpose and met end user requirements.

A teacher at Morgan describes the building as "old and distinguished on the outside, but inside it's spacious, modern and designed to meet the educational needs of the modern society it serves."

Mossbourne Community Academy

London, United Kingdom (England)

Mossbourne Community Academy

London, United Kingdom (England)

Criteria
Flexibility / Sustainability

Architect
Richard Rogers Partnership

Type of School
Lower and upper secondary

No. of Students
420 (rising by 200 each year to
1 000 students by 2009)

Type of Project
New building

Gross Surface Area
8 312 m2

Year of Completion
2004

Client
Mossbourne Community Academy Ltd.

The triangular site of the Mossbourne Community Academy is enclosed on two sides by busy, and noisy, railway tracks. In response, the three-storey building, one of the largest timber-framed structures in the United Kingdom, is conceived as a broad V with its back to the railway tracks and the third side looking out onto the generous external space of Hackney Downs.

Sustainability was one of the key issues addressed in the design and construction of the building from the outset. Existing buildings of the old school were demolished. After removing hazardous materials, the remains were crushed to a structural grade and re-used. Vibro-pile foundations of the building and build-up of the playgrounds were constructed utilising this crushed material.

The building's main frame is built out of glue-laminated timber from a renewable source. This was the most sustainable choice of material for this purpose on its own merits, but it also allowed for better solutions throughout the building. Open plan atria inside the building maximise the use of natural light in the classrooms and circulation areas, improving the quality of the spaces while reducing energy consumption.

Thermal performance is further assisted by the solid wall to the rear of the site, the primary purpose of which is to protect the teaching areas from the negative impact of the railway lines at the back. Although the site produced challenging acoustic conditions, windows and specially designed ventilation towers allow natural ventilation in most areas of the building.

Mossbourne belongs to the government's flagship programme of academies – state schools funded partly by private sponsorship. To become an academy, private sponsors must put up 20% of capital costs, capped at GBP 2 million. Mossbourne Academy is named after the father of its private sponsor, Sir Clive Bourne; the Department for Education and Skills funded the remainder of the project.

Mossbourne Academy is a light, open and airy building with its two arms reaching out to a central open space and Hackney Downs. The architects' innovative design uses traditional materials to provide an attractive learning environment for pupils.

Queen Anne High School
Dunfermline, United Kingdom (Scotland)

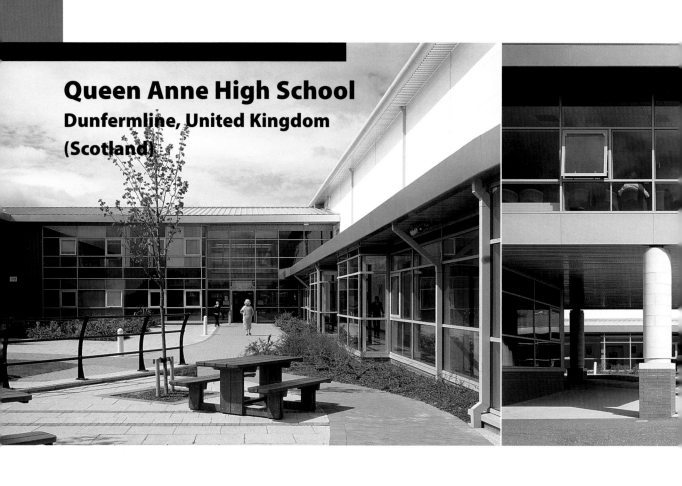

Queen Anne High School
Dunfermline, United Kingdom (Scotland)

Criteria
Community / Finance

Architect
AEDAS

Type of School
Lower and upper secondary

No. of Students
1 758

Type of Project
New building

Gross Surface Area
21 121 m2

Year of Completion
2003

Client
Fife Council

Visitors to the school are impressed by the peaceful environment. But, importantly, it is increasingly an effective learning environment. Senior pupils are using the tutorial rooms well for independent learning. Staff is using the bases to discuss issues of importance. Parents and the wider community are using the facilities for out-of-hours classes and social events, and our performing arts facilities are superb.

Queen Anne High School was the first and largest of Fife's initial set of Public Private Partnership (PPP) schools and is a completely self-contained architectural entity, sited in its own fully developed and landscaped grounds on the northern edge of Dunfermline.

The predominantly two-storey school encompasses the full spectrum of secondary education. The teaching classrooms are distributed by department around four landscaped courtyards. Main pupil circulation moves effectively through the school by the use of a corridor racecourse around the open courtyards.

The main public reception elevations are composed largely of an appealing mix of grey tinted glazed screen walling and warm red brickwork. Elsewhere, the elevational treatment of the school is of human scale and made up of an interesting palette of glazing, bricks, cedar lining, and sandstone faced lintols and cills.

Fife Council, recognising that it did not have the available funding either through capital consents or capital receipts, decided that Queen Anne High School would be rebuilt as part of a wider PPP agreement. Under such arrangements the private sector designs, builds, finances, maintains and operates accommodations which meet the Council's requirements in exchange for an annual revenue payment.

The PPP agreements offer the potential both to improve infrastructure more rapidly and to obtain best value for money when compared to alternative means of procurement. The value for money appraisal undertaken for this project demonstrated that the net present value of the unitary charge payable over the 25-year contract term was 7.3% below the risk adjusted public sector comparator. When considered alongside the technical, legal and other financial merits of the project, the scheme clearly resulted in a value for money solution for Fife Council and a beautiful educational facility for the community.

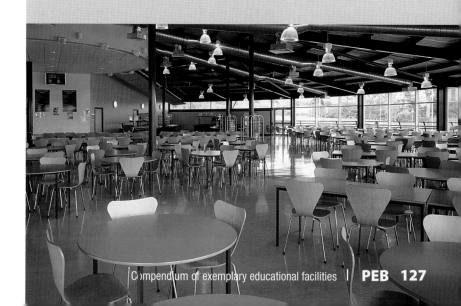

Unlimited Paenga Tawhiti

Christchurch, New Zealand

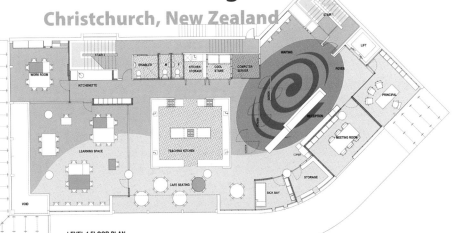

LEVEL 1 FLOOR PLAN

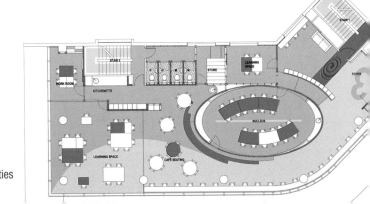

Unlimited Paenga Tawhiti
Christchurch, New Zealand

Criteria
Flexibility / Community / Finance

Architect
Wynyard Design Limited

Type of School
Lower and upper secondary

No. of Students
200

Type of Project
New building

Gross Surface Area
2 050 m2

Year of Completion
2005

Client
Unlimited Paenga Tawhiti Secondary
School

U nlimited Paenga Tawhiti is the first school in New Zealand to be fully financed under the "Cash for Property" scheme, designed to give the Board of Trustees of schools a more direct role in decision-making about the property needs of a school. The Ministry of Education established the capital commitment required to develop this school of 400 in the heart of Christchurch's central business district. This budget figure was then made available to the Board to develop a school that meets the ministry's legislative and policy requirements. Unlimited Paenga Tawhiti leases three adjacent spaces on 12- and 8-year terms. The cost of fit-out was deducted from the figure that the ministry established, and the ongoing costs of the rent and operating expenses are funded by the ministry from an agreed rate of return on the remaining unspent capital it held.

High visibility

With an emphasis on entrepreneurship, technology, and scientific thinking and capability, the facilities have been designed with multipurpose, flexible spaces ranging from single person work stations to areas for 50 or more students. Leading edge technology is included throughout the building, with all hardware leased so that it can be regularly updated.

The interior fit-out has been designed to reveal the technologies associated with the building structure and functioning. This provides a strong interior/exterior link with the extensive use of glass, metal, bold geometric form, natural materials and contrasts which define the exterior of the building. The concept of education being highly visible within the community is evident with the three glass faces of the building and outdoor terraces on two levels with independent work stations.

A genuine partnership

A strong emphasis is placed on interpersonal relationships and a sense of belonging. The significant use of glass in interior walls ensures that there is a high degree of visibility without noise distractions. Because of the attention to acoustic control, noise levels in open areas remain low, making these places popular for students and staff to work individually or in social groups.

In keeping with the school's philosophy of a genuine partnership with students, parents and staff, there are no separate facilities such as a staff room or teacher offices. Staff and students share the range of spaces as suited to the activity they are working on. On each floor of the building, there is a "lunch kitchen" where food and hot drinks can be prepared and shared in a unique social space.

Having staff and students work alongside each other creates a sense of openness and strengthens their relationships. Because of this, students know more about things happening in the school, and there is much more opportunity for their input into decision-making.

Australian Science and Mathematics School

Bedford Park, Australia

The design of the school's learning and physical environments is based on pivotal beliefs about student-centred teaching and learning, lifelong learning, the relevance of science and mathematics to the world's future, the interconnectedness of knowledge, and the importance of human communication in all its forms. The ASMS building offers an ICT rich environment, facilitating learning anywhere and anytime, and opportunities for students from all educational, cultural and socio-economic backgrounds to collaborate with their learning.

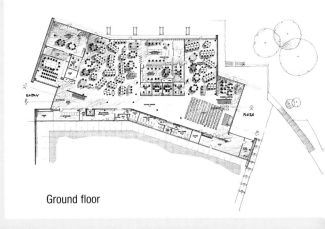

Ground floor

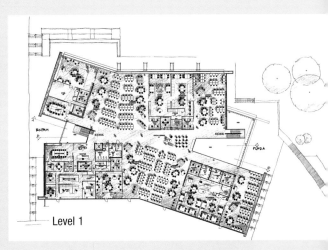

Level 1

Australian Science and Mathematics School
Bedford Park, Australia

Criteria
Flexibility / Sustainability

Architect
Woods Bagot

Type of School
Upper secondary

No. of Students
265

Type of Project
New building

Gross Surface Area
5 010 m2

Year of Completion
2003

Client
Department of Education and Children's Services

The Australian Science and Mathematics School (ASMS) is an innovative, internationally recognised centre for research-based teaching and learning, specialising in sciences and mathematics. Developed jointly between the Department of Education, Training and Employment and Flinders University, the school is designed to be a catalyst for advances in teacher preparation and professional development through education, business and industry partnerships using new and emerging technologies and enterprise initiatives.

Building a learning tool

It was considered important that the building design should incorporate best practice in environmentally sustainable design and intelligent building concepts. Through these concepts, the building itself is a learning tool for the school and enables students to develop an understanding of how buildings, people and the natural environment interact. The output from the building management system is linked to the school's intranet, providing information on the performance of the building's active and passive systems.

The principal features include a state-of-the-art, mixed mode air-conditioning system integrating natural ventilation; a façade incorporating high performance "low emission" glazing and extensive shading elements; dual water reticulation to serve toilet flushing separately and enable reclaimed water to be used for this purpose; and solar boosting of hot water generation via a roof-mounted solar collector.

Changing spaces

Critical to the school's function is the break away from the traditional concepts of classrooms and laboratories. These have been replaced by "learning commons" and "studios". The spaces are designed to be student centred and foster collaborative and project-based learning.

Each student has his or her own "home-base" work station located in one of the learning commons, and the studios are fitted out with specialist services and hands-on facilities to enable students to undertake practical work and experiments which support activities in the learning commons. Flexibility is a key requirement for these areas with several studios set up in pairs with operable walls or partial partitions between to allow interconnection for larger groups. The large central common along with the social and circulation areas are used for exhibitions, assemblies and conferences.

Blyth Community College

Blyth, Northumberland, United Kingdom (England)

Overall, the College is a great place to learn and it gives you the opportunity to make new friends and start new activities.

Blyth Community College
Blyth, Northumberland, United Kingdom (England)

Criteria
Flexibility / Community / Finance

Architect
Waring & Netts

Type of School
Upper secondary

No. of Students
1 400

Type of Project
New building

Gross Surface Area
14 337 m2

Year of Completion
2002

Client
Northumberland County Council

B lyth Community College is an inclusive, creative, county mixed comprehensive school designed to raise student attainment and self esteem while also providing a lifelong learning centre for the community.

Community interaction

The building is designed around the "street", a three-storey high glass-roofed centre-piece to the site. This not only brings light into the heart of the College, it also provides a wonderfully open and airy social centre for the students, teachers and visitors. Circulation between classrooms and access to other common areas is from the "street".

A principal common area is the Open Learning Centre. The Centre houses the college library, the local public library and the ICT facility. The Centre is open to the general public with flexible extended hours, including child care, and offers a wide range of learning opportunities and activities for all ages. Located next to the Cyber Café, it is an outstanding facility that promotes learning and community interaction in a relaxed, welcoming environment. The adult learning programme, for example, has been a terrific success.

Special functions

Another important structure is the auditorium. It provides a flexible performance area with seating for 350 that can be partially or fully stored away to expand the workshop or performance space. The auditorium is the heart of the Performing Arts Department, which includes a music department with three large studios and a half dozen smaller spaces, and a dance studio with a special sprung floor. As one of the best equipped and most versatile such complexes in the region, it is increasing being hired for conferences and other community functions.

Fjölbrautaskóli Snæfellinga
Grundarfjörður, Iceland

Although it is working surprisingly well, the flexibility of the learning environment offers opportunities to achieve an even more effective school in the future that can further enhance student achievement.

Fjölbrautaskóli Snæfellinga
Grundarfjörður, Iceland

Criteria
Flexibility

Architect
VA Architects, Indro Candi and Sigurður Björgúlfsson

Type of School
Upper secondary

No. of Students
110

Type of Project
New building

Gross Surface Area
2 280 m2

Year of Completion
2005

Client
Ministry of Education

Two primary factors were influential in defining the architectural concepts and attributes of this new school building. First, it was decided that the school environment should facilitate new teaching and learning methods with open spaces rather than closed classrooms, where students and teachers can circulate and interact. Secondly, the school is located in a small fishing village in rural Iceland. The building is large in comparison with the scale of the surrounding houses, so it was important for the scale of the village to be reflected in the school building.

In response to these factors, the building is designed as a complex of smaller interconnected units, creating variations of the user's spatial experience and giving each area a distinct character, level of enclosure, acoustic quality and intimacy. Furthermore, the school's exterior harmonises with its surroundings as an aggregated cluster of buildings rather than a single, uniform structure.

New forms of learning spaces for new methods of learning

The architecture of the school is well suited for the form of learning and teaching required and enhances the idea of an open and diverse learning environment designed to accommodate groups of students and teachers with various needs – big spaces, small spaces, open spaces or closed spaces with as much flexibility as possible. The whole school is equipped with a wireless network which enables the students to work on their assignments wherever in the school they choose, individually or in groups.

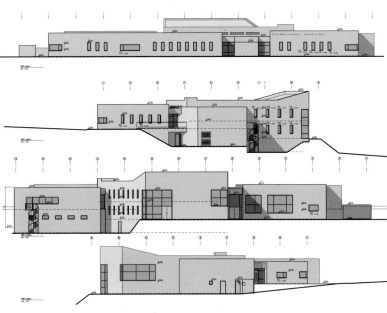

Gymnase du Bugnon – Site de Sévelin
Lausanne, Switzerland

Gymnase du Bugnon – Site de Sévelin
Lausanne, Switzerland

Criteria
Sustainability

Architect
CCHE Architecture, S.A.

Type of School
Upper secondary

No. of Students
450

Type of Project
Renovation

Gross Surface Area
3 860 m2

Year of Completion
2004

Client
HG Commerciale

This school building is the result of the extensive and carefully planned renovation of a former warehouse, originally constructed in 1930, and meets the expectations of the users. The teachers and students appreciate the spaces, the light and the urban location, while the sustainable design and energy efficiency of the building add to its function.

Strong foundation for renewed purpose

The original concrete exterior, avant-garde for its time, has been kept fully intact. The structure of the building is also unchanged, although the addition of a top floor was seriously considered. In addition, a large number of the components of the building were repaired, re-used or recycled (*e.g.* tiles, ironwork, stonework). Located in a constantly changing industrial district, the new school utilises the best features of the original building while adding many key features of its own.

The pure and simple design concept focuses on the numerous and harmonious open areas. The arrangement of space and specialty rooms was planned with the teachers, in particular, the music room, library, laboratories and creative activities rooms. Stairways and common areas are designed to maximise the space and circulation between classrooms. The most eye-catching aspect may be the vast skylights that have been installed, creating light corridors that assure better general distribution of natural light throughout the building.

The renovation was completed within the strict standards required for the MINERGIE certification. This confirms that the building follows energy efficient criteria in relation to energy consumption, air quality, natural lighting and protection from exterior noise.

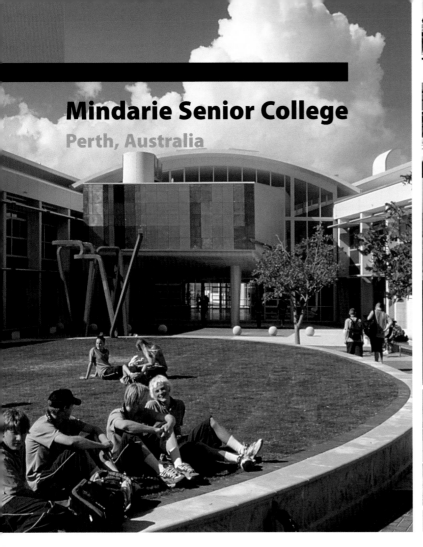

Mindarie Senior College
Perth, Australia

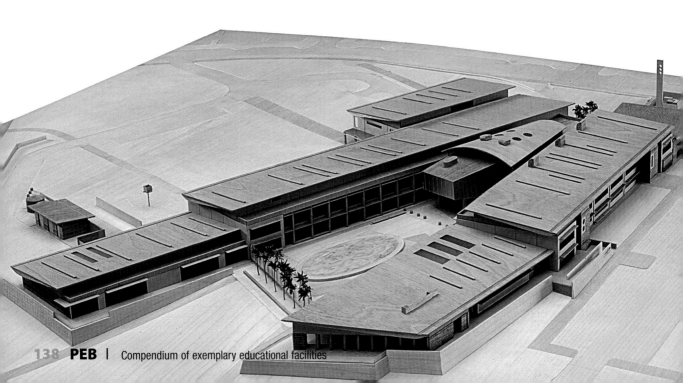

Mindarie Senior College
Perth, Australia

Criteria
Flexibility / Community / Sustainability

Architect
Dick Donaldson, Donaldson + Warn, Architects

Type of School
Upper secondary

No. of Students
560

Type of Project
New building

Gross Surface Area
8 500 m2

Year of Completion
2003

Client
Department of Education and Training/Housing and Works

The building is just awesome, there is so much space, and you have these cool views of the ocean and all these colours make you feel so much more energetic. It is a great place to learn. It's not like a normal school when you feel drained at the end of the day and can't wait to get home. At Mindarie you feel energised.

The spatial and architectural image of Mindarie Senior College is something like a holistic "institute of learning", reflecting the trend toward acknowledging the young adult stage of secondary schooling. The building is designed as a mature learning environment where all areas promote educational and social interaction with cross fertilisation of ideas across curriculum areas, rather than a more traditional combination of different building blocks of specialist faculties.

Maximising the location

The singularly significant aspect is, in both educational and architectural terms, to move from a number of individualised teaching blocks, dedicated to specific learning areas and separated by courtyards and walkways, to a single building envelope. All the learning areas relate directly to each other and are held together by a central atrium and courtyard.

The building incorporates a variety of formal and informal learning spaces and social spaces for student and student/staff interaction. It takes advantage of the site's spectacular elevated location and is designed to reflect its coastal context and maximise passive environmental control systems.

The site is located approximately 700 metres from the Indian Ocean on the crest of a limestone hill, the highest point in the surrounding area. The building makes references to its seaside context and reflects the nature of the surrounding environment through its planning, form, detail, material and colour. The atrium and external courtyard is the central focus and conceived as one continuous space with views westerly to the ocean and easterly to the Darling Ranges. The two accommodation wings on either side of the atrium exploit the cross flow ventilation benefits of the prevailing sea breezes. Further responses to the challenge presented by the wind and other environmental conditions include a glazed screen and wind scoops to deflect and channel the breeze, passive roof ventilators, and sunshade canopies over all the windows.

The school is predominantly two-storey with an internal circulation spine, which acts not only as weather protection to this exposed site but as a social conduit and an interactive learning space. The circulation spine incorporates computer alcoves that can be used for individual study or group work. At first floor level, the circulation widens to form an open non dedicated space in the atrium that has been provided for informal learning opportunities. Teaching spaces are designed as an assortment of different sized and shaped rooms that can be combined or separated to suit class size. This spatial customisation gives both teachers and students a sense of ownership and control over their environment.

Berufsschule für Gartenbau und Floristik
Vienna, Austria

Berufsschule für Gartenbau und Floristik
Vienna, Austria

Criteria
Sustainability

Architect
Atelier 4 Architects

Type of School
Tertiary

No. of Students
600

Type of Project
New building

Gross Surface Area
8 587 m2

Year of Completion
2002

Client
Provincial Government of Vienna

Energy plays a particularly important role at this vocational school of horticulture and floristry. It is the energy of light, water, air and soil that forms the basis for plant growth, and the innovative architecture of this building plays a decisive role in this regard. The building itself becomes a teaching tool for creating a sustainable, energy efficient living environment.

Pedagogical design concept

The school was designed as a pavilion and thematic school, positioned between park grounds on one side and horticultural fields on the other. The building itself is designed to be not just a shell for the conveyance of theoretical knowledge but also a means to demonstrate and experiment in the various subjects in the field of horticulture and floristry. The main body of the building opens up onto the park and is partially roofed over, thereby giving a more concrete form to the airiness that is expected of a pavilion.

At the second floor, the building is penetrated by a magnificent plateau-like open space as an extension of the park to the east. This inner courtyard garden, together with the roof plateau and vertical garden of the façade, provides exhibition surfaces for specific topics of instruction in the school. The roof itself is a showcase of different roof garden models and systems. A central atrium flooded with light from above is the heart and access hub of the facility, and is also a venue for testing and designing indoor plant elements. The botanical "showcase" theme of the entrance and connecting path presents visitors with the contents of the curriculum, and confirms the image of the school as a venue of urban cohesion.

Alternative energy measures

A careful management of energy and resources is an important educational mission of the school. Generally, the facility's engineering is designed to be as simple as possible. These systems are composed of ecological heating from building components (radiant panel heating), photovoltaic installations and lines of non-potable water used for toilet flushing and watering the gardens.

Moreover, an air intake and ventilation system has been incorporated into the classrooms as an object of testing and research for a new concept in air-conditioning. Under the motto "Good Air for Good Students", several classrooms are equipped with downstream ventilation. A healthier learning environment has improved students' concentration and attentiveness.

Cégep de Sainte-Foy

Sainte-Foy, Canada

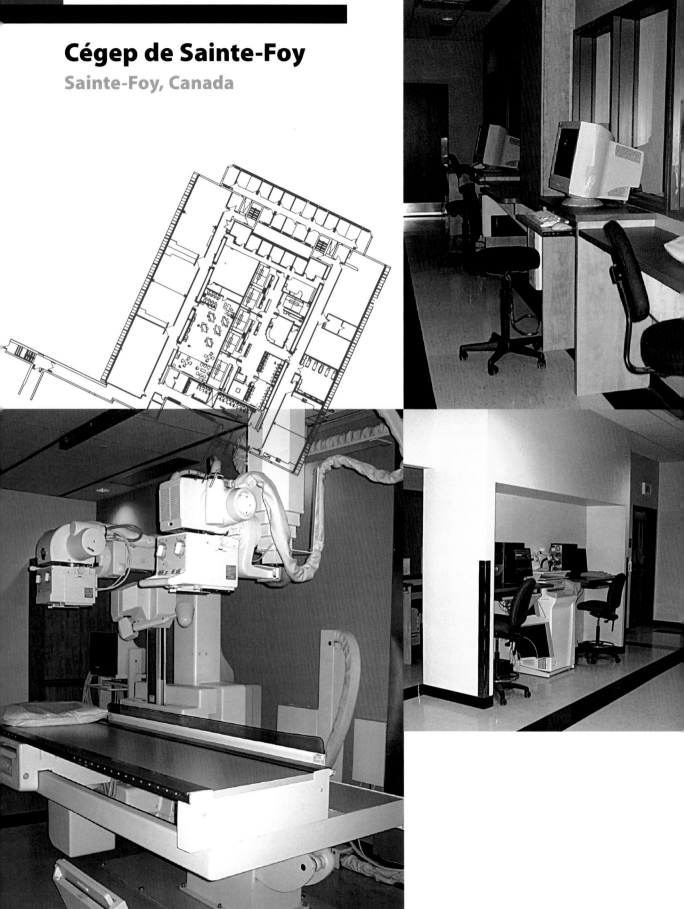

Cégep de Sainte-Foy
Sainte-Foy, Canada

Criteria
Security

Architect
Bélanger, Beauchemin Architectes

Type of School
Tertiary

No. of Students
180

Type of Project
Extension

Gross Surface Area
1 065 m2

Year of Completion
2004

Client
Cégep de Sainte-Foy, Département de Radiodiagnostic

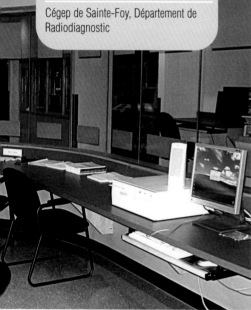

This facility has been designed for the study of radio diagnostic technology. The learning environment for this highly specialised field is centred on state-of-the-art equipment and an exemplary organisation of space. The creation of a laboratory area without a corridor effect, where movement is incorporated into the layout and where service alcoves are preferred to closed rooms, gives the facility a highly professional character where all the space is used to its full potential.

Interaction between practice and theory

The overall design was conceived to provide students with effective means of achievement. The commitment to an exemplary learning context where the student as well as the technician and teacher benefit is reflected in the quality of the equipment, the use of the latest technology, and even the installation of unique programmes such as SIMULIX (a computerised radiological examination simulation programme accessible via Internet) and PACS (a system of storage of several thousand digitalised radiological images). This environment was conceived by and for the users, and throughout the facility one is aware of the effort to integrate with the labour market and to align training and professional practice.

The very nature of the teaching programme for radio diagnostic technology demands constant interaction between practice and theory. Thus all areas of the department, including the teachers' offices, are arranged around and even within the laboratory space so that students and teachers are constantly at the heart of the clinical environment. Likewise, the installation of different types of radiology equipment initiates students in the various technologies to be found in professional practice. The protected observation areas are spacious so as to allow simultaneous observation and practice, maximising the use of the costly equipment.

Specialist environment for professional students

The choice of the site for the extension, an interior court on the second floor of the building, to some extent forced the concentration of the facilities in a central core, and the advantages are palpable at all levels. On entering the department, one immediately feels transported into a specialist environment, and the architectural language is constant throughout. This undoubtedly contributes to the seriousness and professionalism shown by the students.

This arrangement also encourages respect for equipment. The sense of entering a highly specialist area where so much quality equipment is available to the students undoubtedly makes them more responsible and respectful, and even proud.

Centre de Formation des Nouvelles Technologies

Sainte-Thérèse, Canada

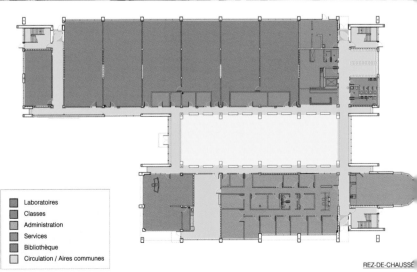

- Laboratoires
- Classes
- Administration
- Services
- Bibliothèque
- Circulation / Aires communes

REZ-DE-CHAUSSÉ

Commission scolaire de la Seigneurie-des-Mille-Îles / Bouré Therrien L'Ecuyer Lefaivre / Hamelin Lalonde / Birtz Bastien architectes

Centre de Formation des Nouvelles Technologies
Sainte-Thérèse, Canada

Criteria
Flexibility / Community / Security

Architect
Bouré Therrien L'Ecuyer Lefaivre, Hamelin Lalonde, Birtz Bastien

Type of School
Tertiary

No. of Students
600 full-time, 400 part-time

Type of Project
New building

Gross Surface Area
6 880 m2

Year of Completion
2003

Client
Philippe Lalande, Commission Scolaire de la Seigneurie-des-Mille-Iles

The construction of the New Technologies Training Centre building is noteworthy in several ways. Designed to enhance vocational training in education by providing a stimulating environment and setting comparable to a workplace, the building itself becomes a tool conducive to the success of its students in the pursuit of their educational goals.

Set at the south-west corner of a site which already accommodates two existing municipal buildings (a library and multi-service centre), the new building benefits from the existing structures and integrates into the urban framework. Following the same angle as the existing buildings, it forms an enclosed court at the rear. The alignment on the site allows re-use of existing access and parking, resulting in savings which could be re-allocated to the architecture.

Linear organisation

The life of the building, its physical and functional heart is the atrium. A characteristic and distinctive element for a vocational training facility, the atrium is located at the centre and is open on three levels. It provides a social meeting place for teachers and students, and is also used for exhibitions and community events. The atrium is surrounded by walkways forming mezzanines that lead to the teaching sectors.

Each sector, or teaching programme, is organised as a series of modules, so that the workshop, theory class, movement and services can be divided and re-arranged. These modules are laid out in linear fashion along the corridors of the building. The repetitive arrangement of the modules becomes the conceptual framework of the building. The sectors are organised horizontally as well as vertically from floor to floor, as autonomous entities around the centre.

A firm concept

The concept of the centre is more like a firm than a traditional school. Putting all vocational education programmes together in one building allows students from all backgrounds to intermingle, talk, meet and confirm their choice of vocation.

The distinct technological image of the building itself, inspired by transparency, luminescence and natural light, creates an atmosphere that is particularly conducive to work. The architecture and design promotes top-quality training to meet the demands of the labour market and creates a sense of belonging and pride among all its users.

Collège Shawinigan
Shawinigan, Canada

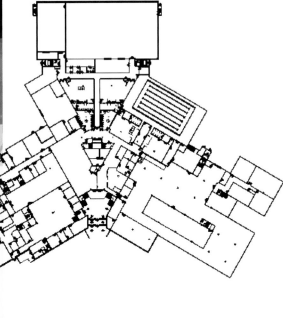

Collège Shawinigan
Shawinigan, Canada

Criteria
Flexibility / Community / Sustainability / Security

Architect
Les Architectes Michel Pellerin, Sylvie Rainville, Renée Tremblay

Type of School
Tertiary

No. of Students
1 200 full-time, 250 part-time

Type of Project
Renovation

Gross Surface Area
2 033 m2

Year of Completion
2004

Client
Collège Shawinigan

The terms which best characterise the effectiveness of the Hub are: accessibility, visibility, luminosity, dissemination, good content and infinite future possibilities.

One word describes the idea, the essence of the educational and architectural project at the heart of the renovation and transformation of the Shawinigan College library into the Desjardins Information Hub: openness.

The heart of the College

The library was already located at the heart of the College, but scarcely visible. The project's educational and architectural approach was to create a true intersection of knowledge and learning centres.

The area is arranged around a central feature in the shape of a four-pointed star symbolising the dream of success. The four points are visible on the floor and ceiling indicating the main entrance, the view over the city and community, the library and media section, and teaching resources.

The Hub provides an up-to-date technological infrastructure. It is equipped with a wireless information network which allows students, teachers and staff with a suitably configured portable computer to work on their projects in the comfort of the Hub.

The area is also equipped with a state-of-the-art multi-media room used for training in documentary research by students and in information technology by teachers and staff, as well as being available for hire by firms in the region.

Effectiveness and efficiency

The design is based on a functional programme and an innovative method. The use of materials, shapes and colours and the interplay of space with the maximum use of natural light adds to the beauty of the area and the attraction of this unique community space. The pursuit of effectiveness and efficiency in the service to the users is the predominant element.

Grouping a set of support and ancillary services in the same environment enhances its potential adaptability to accommodate all activities. The state-of-the-art computer equipment completes the mission of openness and accessibility to knowledge among the target users and the community. This achievement was made possible thanks to the involvement of the community in the campaign to finance the Shawinigan College Foundation. The building of the Desjardins Information Hub was the major project of that campaign.

Georgetown University
Law Center

Washington, D.C., United States

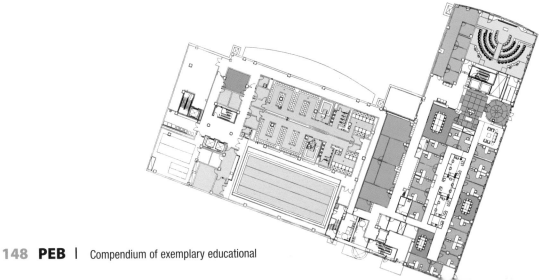

Georgetown University Law Center
Washington, D.C., United States

Criteria
Community / Security

Architect
Shepley Bullfinch Richardson and Abbott

Type of School
Tertiary

No. of Students
1 862 full-time, 490 part-time

Type of Project
New building

Gross Surface Area
4 720 m2

Year of Completion
2004

Client
Georgetown University Law Center

The nature of legal education is changing. At one time, law courses were taught in large classrooms using the Socratic Method. Today, clinical legal education, simulation, problem-solving and small class discussion methods are complementing traditional pedagogy and will, in the future, overtake it. The Eric E. Hotung International Law Building provides two new medium-sized classrooms and ten small classrooms to accommodate these changes. Moreover, the new pedagogy makes greater use of interactive technology.

The planning goals for the Hotung International Law Building were to foster a sense of community among students, faculty and administration and to create an oasis within the confined urban environment of the campus. The project was designed to enhance a sense of communal identity by creating an exterior civic space and interior public spaces with opportunities for learning and interaction.

High-tech facilities

Law schools exist to provide future attorneys with the theoretical and practical fundamentals to launch them into their careers and to provide a base from which lifelong learning will prevail. The design of both law firms and courts has changed dramatically in the past ten years and the Hotung International Law Building creatively responds to these changes. Wireless communication systems, flexible classrooms, and two high-tech courtroom/classrooms equipped with annotation screen computers, document cameras, plasma screens, video capability and courtroom control from the judge's bench replicate the courtrooms found in U.S. Courts. In addition, one of these courtroom/classrooms replicates the United States Supreme Court so that litigators can prepare their arguments in a setting that resembles the actual Court.

The classrooms in the Hotung Building provide the most advanced classroom technology in the U.S. legal academy. Classrooms are equipped with smart podia; computers, DVD and tape capability; and projection screens and Smart Boards. Also, the entire campus is equipped with wireless communications systems so that students can conduct group discussions, access the library, and contact their professors at any time.

The goal was to design a building of restrained elegance that proclaimed the intention to pursue global academic excellence without appearing aloof. It signifies the need to nurture academic life, but also to contribute to life along the street, to be part of an urban neighbourhood and of an ever-more integrated world. The building succeeds dramatically. The building is about people, democracy and accessibility and not about the sometimes rigid strictures of academic hierarchies.

Kaposvári Egyetem
Kaposvár, Hungary

Kaposvári Egyetem
Kaposvár, Hungary

Criteria
Flexibility

Architect
Dezsö Töreky

Type of School
Tertiary

No. of Students
1 667 full-time, 1 977 part-time

Type of Project
New building

Gross Surface Area
6 500 m2

Year of Completion
2004

Client
Kaposvári Egyetem

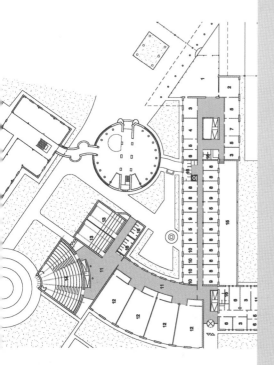

The planning and design of the new buildings for the University of Kaposvár were carried out totally by means of computer technology. All areas of planning, such as building engineering, electric and IT networks, monitoring and controlling networks, and the total audiovisual system were designed using computer modelling. This modern planning approach not only provided a basis for combining different designs and carrying out the optimal solutions safely, it is also suitable for monitoring and correcting the operation of different technical systems while the building is used.

Diverse designs

The main purpose in the planning was to create multiple types of lecture halls and seminar rooms for the individual professional groups of different sizes, with the capacity of 25 to 250 people, including music practice rooms, drawing studios, and chemistry, physics, biology and nutrition laboratories. The rooms are equipped with the latest audiovisual technology. The diversity of the rooms in terms of size and fields of study facilitates the present and future use of modern educational technologies.

One of the main principles included in the architectural concept was to create a human-centred, architecturally authentic building complex that satisfies the needs of the students in the most effective way. The characteristics of the site and the professional demands required a versatile and dynamic architectural design. The new multi-purpose buildings match the landscape, the existing buildings and each other, contributing both functionally and aesthetically to the prestige of the university.

In the laboratory

An important area in the new building is the Molecular Biology Laboratory. Its planning and construction provide the conditions necessary for fulfilling its functions both as a place of learning and as a centre for research in molecular genetics. A wireless IT network is available throughout the facility. The laboratory furniture is easy to handle, and the appliances can be connected to water outlets and the electrical system in the floor. The storage room contains sanitary units and is also equipped with an exhaust system for handling hazardous chemicals. The ventilation system and the high-brilliance, economical lights also contribute to the convenience of users and the effectiveness of their work.

National Maritime College
Cork, Ireland

National Maritime College
Cork, Ireland

Criteria
Flexibility / Community / Sustainability

Architect
Building Design Partnership

Type of School
Tertiary

No. of Students
300 full-time, 150 part-time

Type of Project
New building

Gross Surface Area
14 000 m2

Year of Completion
2004

Client
Department of Education and Science

The National Maritime College is located on a reclaimed foreshore on the estuary of the River Lee adjacent to the Irish Naval Service Headquarters at Haulbowline. The building accommodates 750 full-time equivalent students with state-of-the-art training simulators, classrooms, laboratories and workshops. A diver training tank and helicopter "dunker" pool are also incorporated adjacent to a new slipway and jetty, and staff and students can take advantage of the fitness training and gymnasium facilities within the complex.

Towards the water

A dramatic, slicing, cedar clad wall celebrates the arrival and the very identity of the College. The entrance arrangement includes a linear walkway and boardwalk leading to a two-storey glazed entrance atrium. The water feature continues past the atrium into the more informal landscape to the rear leading the eye out to the sea and beyond.

Organised in three articulated "fingers" of accommodation around the separate functions within the College, the complex stretches towards the water, capturing dramatic views which are never allowed to be far from the student experience of the curriculum. The engineering profile of the building is an important design principle, and the scheme was developed with particular emphasis on using passive means of controlling the internal environment where possible.

Advanced thermal modelling was utilised to develop the building cross section that ensures adequate air flows through the teaching and administration blocks. Natural ventilation to control the environment is assisted by a thermally heavy structure with extensive exposed surfaces. This is an important factor not only in terms of reducing operating costs but also responding to obvious environmental issues.

The brief for the building was developed between the Department of Education and Science, the Irish Naval Service, Cork Institute of Technology, and Focus Education (Ireland) Ltd. to meet the new international training requirements for civil and naval (non-military) seafarers and took the form of a detailed output specification. The College and its design team used the output specification and ordered the complex series of requirements: from full bridge simulators to marine engine workshops; from sea survival and fire training requirements to the learning resource centre; from freefall craft to lecture theatre and specialist training rooms. The result is an exciting, vibrant and stimulating building which provides facilities to meet the training requirements with a highly functional and imaginative solution.

National University of Ireland, Maynooth

Maynooth, Co. Kildare, Ireland

**National University of
Ireland, Maynooth**
Maynooth, Co. Kildare, Ireland

Criteria
Flexibility / Community / Sustainability

Architect
Coady Partnership Architects

Type of School
Tertiary

No. of Students
4 500 full-time, 600 part-time

Type of Project
New building

Gross Surface Area
5 700 m2

Year of Completion
2004

Client
NUI Maynooth

The John Hume Building lies at the fulcrum of the master plan for the north campus at NUI Maynooth. It provides a new four-storey central teaching facility for a number of faculties including the Department of Psychology and acts as the main research base of the university.

From the outset, the design team set themselves the challenge of designing a building which would be fully naturally vented and make as much use of passive ventilation, heating and lighting as possible, resulting in lower running costs for the university and substantially reduced CO_2 emissions.

Outstanding facilities

The building is organised around a linear atrium, with the main teaching spaces comprising three auditoria at ground floor. The atrium is raversed with a route linking the two main entrances and provides easy access to students arriving from both ends of the campus. Student facilities including a bookshop, bank, restaurant and other services are located at ground floor, accessed from the main concourse. The Psychology Department occupies the third floor, with laboratories to one side and offices on the other. The fourth floor provides studios for post-doctoral research and other resource areas for visiting lecturers and research staff.

Naturally efficient ventilation

The main lecture theatres are naturally ventilated with assisted mechanical extract, controlled to switch on as CO_2 and temperature levels rise. Low velocity extract ducts from the two smaller lecture theatres are expressed as coloured tubes rising through the main atrium. In a similar way the natural ventilation and heating within the theatres are dramatically expressed by slatted timber panelling, profiled ceilings and slots below the tiered seating designed to allow the passage of air.

The atrium plays a central role in the natural ventilation strategy. Its height makes it possible to draw air from the adjacent spaces and to exhaust it at high level. Air from the tutorial rooms and lecture theatres at first floor is vented directly through the rooms to the atrium via continuous louvered grilles and custom-designed plenum boxes to provide vital acoustic and fire separation and is exhausted naturally at roof level.

Ngalilwara Study Centre

Batchelor, Australia

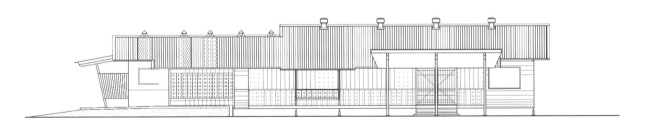

Ngalilwara Study Centre
Batchelor, Australia

Criteria
Flexibility / Community

Architect
Build Up Design Architects Pty. Ltd.

Type of School
Tertiary

No. of Students
60 part-time

Type of Project
New building

Gross Surface Area
7 700 m2

Year of Completion
2002

Client
Batchelor Institute of Indigenous
Tertiary Education

Batchelor Institute of Indigenous Tertiary Education is working with remote Aboriginal communities in Australia's Northern Territory to define appropriate learning spaces that serve their cultural, social and economic needs. Though much work remains to be done, the Institute's efforts have already yielded results by providing an architectural identity that reflects the values and culture of the Indigenous people from the Ngukurr Region in the Northern Territory. Tertiary education enrolments have increased since the Ngalilwara Study Centre was built in Ngukurr.

Empowering the community

The Ngalilwara Batchelor Study Centre in a remote location some 650 km from Darwin provides required learning spaces that are not available elsewhere community-based education leading to employment. Rarely would students have a study space or computer in their own homes. The building provides space for learning and using up-to-date information technology equipment with Internet access and distance learning through the use of a satellite dish.

The Centre comprises two class/lecture rooms with a folding wall dividing the two spaces which can be opened up to one large area. On occasion the room must be divided when, for cultural reasons, two people are not allowed to be in the same room at the same time. Along one wall of both classrooms runs an alcove which houses the computers and associated equipment, and at one end of the double room is a small library. A staff office opens off the classrooms.

Extensive consultation was held with the students and other stakeholders; meetings were conducted in the community over several years and respected cultural sensitivities. Care was taken to ensure that all stakeholders had a voice in the project and that their needs were considered. Since construction of the building the community has continued to take care of the Study Centre.

Two principles underpin all aspects of the Institute's life. Firstly cultural interaction and cross-cultural learning follow a "both ways" philosophy which enables exploration of traditional Aboriginal knowledge and Western academic disciplinary positions and cultural contexts. Secondly through its work and its courses, the Institute affirms aspirations to self-determination and employment held by Aboriginal and Torres Strait Islander people. The Ngalilwara Study Centre enables tertiary education and training to be held in the Community of Ngukurr, students enjoy using the spaces that they have had a role in determining and the result is more educated people which leads to employment and empowerment.

Nyíregyházi Föiskola
Nyíregyháza, Hungary

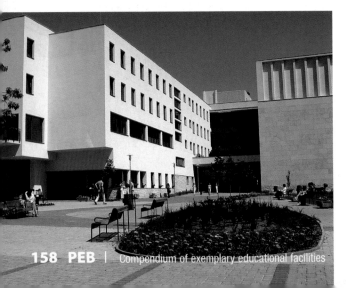

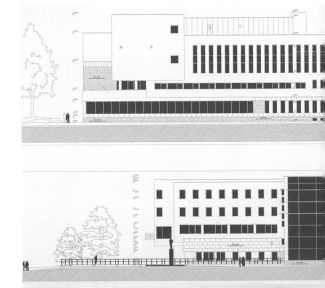

Nyíregyházi Föiskola
Nyíregyháza, Hungary

Criteria
Community

Architect
A Stúdió Kft

Type of School
Tertiary

No. of Students
5 050 full-time, 9 000 part-time

Type of Project
New building

Gross Surface Area
9 132 m2

Year of Completion
2003

Client
Nyíregyházi Föiskola

The mayor is pleased and said, "The College of Nyíregyháza is the pride of the city."

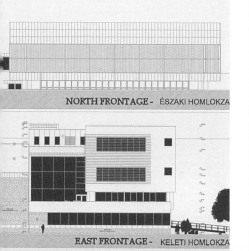

NORTH FRONTAGE - ÉSZAKI HOMLOKZA

EAST FRONTAGE - KELETI HOMLOKZA

The College of Nyíregyháza was established in January 2000 by the merger of the two predecessor institutions: György Bessenyei Teacher Training College and the Agricultural College, Faculty of Gödöllő University. The College now has four faculties: Science, Engineering and Agriculture, Economics/Social Science and Arts.

In September 2003 the new building of the Learning and Information Centre was opened, housing the rector's offices, central library, student registry and financial department. Within a year, the Faculty of Engineering and Agriculture moved into its new premises. At the moment a new block is under construction to provide extra residence for students.

An information hub

The Learning and Information Centre with 250 modern computers and free Internet access helps the students with their studies, research and investigation while providing a central hub for campus information and activity. Every facility and office in this building has high efficiency computers with large databases and other ICT systems, which serve the students and the management of the College. The Bessenyei Aula (large hall in the building) also has a modern ICT system. It can accommodate 800 people and is suitable for organising international meetings and conferences.

Opening opportunities

The construction of the new building allowed the College to accept more students and to create new fields of study. The new facility has become an organic part of the old building complex while creating a more campus-like atmosphere for the College.

The College offers flexible hours to its students and also shares its facilities with the community. On weekdays and Saturdays, the Learning and Information Centre remains open until 10 p.m. During this time lectures are held and the library is available not only to the students, but to anyone who wants to use its services.

The College of Nyíregyháza also has sports facilities unique among Hungarian higher education institutions: a horse riding facility, a swimming pool, a sauna, an athletic hall, sports fields and tracks, and a gymnasium – all in close proximity to the Sóstó Forest.

St. John Ambulance Provincial Headquarters

Edmonton, Canada

St. John nourishes the conscience, showing us how to build in a manner that combines beauty, functionality, and a deep respect for the environment.

St. John Ambulance Provincial Headquarters
Edmonton, Canada

Criteria
Community / Sustainability / Security

Architect
Myron Nebozuk, Manasc Isaac
Architects Ltd.

Type of School
Tertiary

No. of Students
250 part-time

Type of Project
New building

Gross Surface Area
3 400 m2

Year of Completion
2004

Client
St. John Council for Alberta

The new St. John Ambulance Provincial Headquarters is designed to use 48% less energy and 55% less water than most school buildings in Canada. The project takes advantage of energy-efficient walls, windows and roof, as well as low-flow water closets, waterless urinals and no ground irrigation to significantly reduce its impact on energy and water resources. During construction, over 90% of the waste was diverted from landfill. All interior materials were installed without volatile organic compound, leading to a healthy indoor environment. St. John Ambulance Provincial Headquarters was among the first buildings in Canada to achieve the LEED™ Silver designation from the US Green Building Council.

Symbolic design

This building was carefully sited in a run-down urban area that needed revitalisation. It was designed to create a remarkable presence for St. John Ambulance and to symbolise the past, present and future of this 900-year-old community organisation. The medieval tower to the west, complete with circular concrete exit stair, represents the rich history of the Order of St. John. The central classroom portion of the building symbolises the active present – teaching first aid and training community members for better health and safety. The atrium represents birth and renewal – facing east toward the rising sun and acting as the lungs of this naturally-ventilated building, as well as the beacon and gathering place.

Community commitment

Building users were intensely involved in the integrated design and construction process, from initial space planning and programming, to establishing the vision and the details for this building through the User Steering Committee. This group represented staff and students as well as administration and Board members. Weekly workshops and meetings kept people engaged with design decisions at all stages.

Community members share the facility. St. John has a large corps of volunteers, known as the "Brigade", who provide first aid services at local events. There are also a number of programmes operating from this facility which introduce youth to voluntary first aid and community service.

"With the energy efficient and environmental design of the facility, we are committed to a healthy exchange between the operation of our facility and the community we serve," states David Hook, CEO, St. John Council for Alberta.

Szegedi Tudományegyetem Tanulmányi és Infomációs Központ
Szeged, Hungary

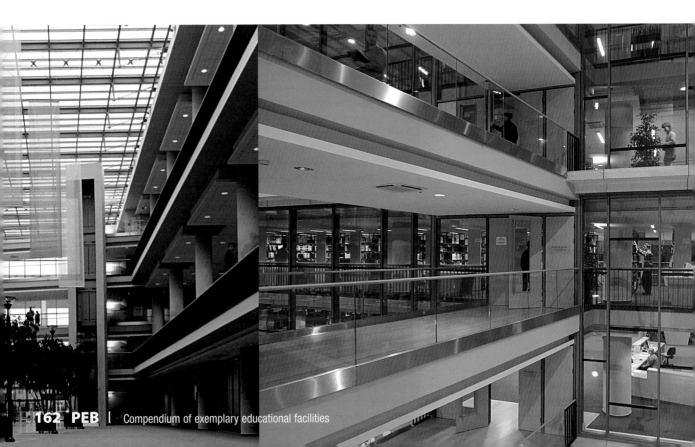

Szegedi Tudományegyetem Tanulmányi és Infomációs Központ
Szeged, Hungary

Criteria
Community

Architect
László Mikó and Tibor Szántó, Szántó & Mikó Architects Ltd.

Type of School
Tertiary

No. of Students
4 000 capacity

Type of Project
New building

Gross Surface Area
25 300 m2

Year of Completion
2004

Client
Ministry of Education

The University of Szeged Study and Information Centre is designed as a learning environment for the future. The concept of the new Centre's building reflects the belief that educational spaces are increasingly freer, more open, complex and changeable. The study environment is unbound too, as the process of learning has become less formal and more individualised. Likewise, the spaces are more open to allow students to circulate easily between them. Facilities are more complex in order to provide for many forms of information and communications: printed and digital, visual and audio, recorded and live, passive and interactive. Finally, the learning environment is more changeable to keep up with innovations in the methods and tools of learning.

The University of Szeged Study and Information Centre contributes to this vision. Its spaces are large and transparent, freely accessible, with the events and activities of the interior and exterior constantly visible. They are also lightly structured to accommodate a variety of activities, with subtle divisions separating them. The facility is equipped with a technical network that provides flexibility in space and time.

The University of Szeged Study and Information Centre is visited by about 4 000 people every day, 70% of whom are university students. It is also a venue for conferences and special programmes; more than 20 000 people took part in over 120 programmes in just six months after the opening. Those in charge of the University and the Centre were involved in the planning and development of the new building, taking the users' experience into consideration. The design and infrastructure of the Centre are an important success for the University, encapsulating a commitment to a dynamic, inventive and vibrant learning environment for the future.

Université du Québec à Montréal

Montreal, Canada

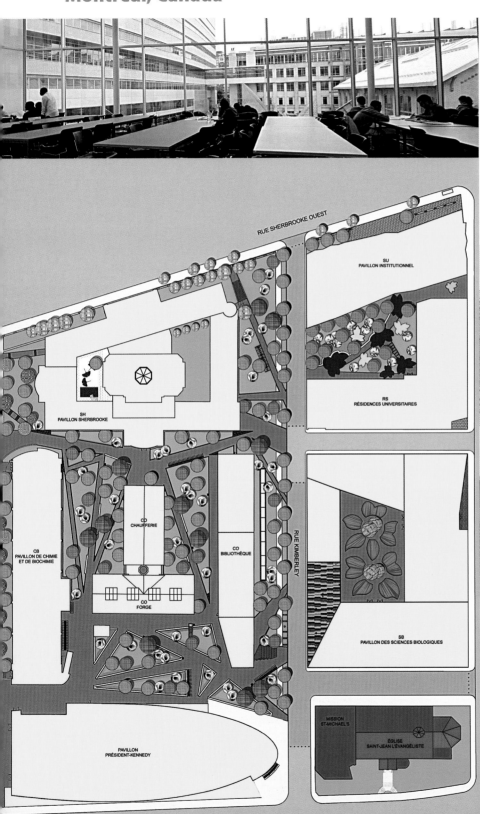

Université du Québec à Montréal
Montreal, Canada

Criteria

Flexibility / Community / Sustainability / Finance

Architect

Tétreault Parent Languedoc et Associés / Saia Barbarese Architectes

Type of School

Tertiary

No. of Students

21 525 full-time, 19 982 part-time

Type of Project

New building

Gross Surface Area

80 462 m2

Year of Completion

2005

Client

Université du Québec à Montréal

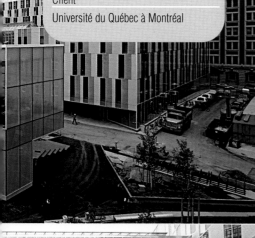

The Biological Sciences Building is one of the last three new buildings to be added to the Science Complex at the University of Quebec in Montreal (UQAM), along with the residence halls and the Administration Building. The Complex also comprises three newly restored historical buildings and three others recently built. New gardens surround all of the buildings, blending them into one cohesive whole while at the same time opening up the site to the heart of the city and to the cultural hub of Montreal.

Form of function

The return of the Biology Department to the Science Complex site had been long awaited. The main development theme for the new spiral shaped Biological Sciences Building was transparency. The spiral is reminiscent of the DNA helix and opens the building to the campus along a pedestrian street. The treatment of the façade is intended to reflect the function of the building, which houses the life sciences. The highest part of the building reaches 11 storeys including its two underground levels.

The construction project for the Biological Sciences Building has been registered with the US Green Building Council in order to obtain certification as a "green building" under the Leadership in Energy and Environmental Design (LEED) system. From the very beginning of the project, the UQAM's goal was to incorporate as many of the LEED rating system criteria as its budget constraints would allow. For example, special attention is paid to storm water management. The design aims to optimise indoor air quality, the energy performance of the building envelope and its air processing systems. In selecting building materials, first preference was given to recycled materials. The building's interior gardens have native plants which do not require a great deal of water. The gardens also serve as a teaching laboratory.

Linking the community

More than a construction challenge, the completion of the UQAM Science Complex in the centre of the city was an intellectual challenge that made it possible for the university to unite knowledge with culture. Moving the Biology Department to its new location in the Biological Sciences Building fosters interdisciplinary links with the whole of the scientific community, particularly in the fields of the environment, biochemistry and biotechnology, and contributes to better working and studying conditions for the department. The landscaped gardens of the Science Complex provide a genuine living environment for students, professors, researchers, support staff and the surrounding community. The addition of university halls of residence enables students to benefit from this environment.

Learning and Learning Spaces

Mary Hanafin T.D.

Minister for
Education and Science

The Government of Ireland continues to invest record funding in its infrastructure, addressing historical deficit, and in the supply of new stock. We are acutely aware of the responsibility this spending brings with it, in ensuring that quality space emerges to the benefit of pupils and staff alike. While value for money remains a key objective for us, research continues to point to close linkages between quality space and learning outcomes.

In this context, the Department of Education and Science continues to engage with practitioners and stakeholders in exploring innovation in teaching and learning, and indeed is a strong contributor on the international stage through its global links in education.

Department of Education and Science
An Roinn Oideachais Agus Eolaíochta

Marlborough Street
Dublin 1
Tel: 00353 1 889 6400

Email: info@education.gov.ie
Web: www.education.ie

AN ROINN
OIDEACHAIS
AGUS EOLAÍOCHTA | DEPARTMENT OF
EDUCATION
AND SCIENCE

Arabian Peruskoulu
P.O. Box 3315
Helsinki, 00099
Finland
Tel: +358 9 3108 7230
Email: kaisu.karkkainen@edu.hel.fi
Web site: www.edu.hel.fi

Ardscoil Mhuire
Mackney, Ballinasloe
Co. Galway
Ireland
Tel: +353 90 964 2206
Email: ardscoilmhuire@eircom.net
Web site: www.ardscoilmhuire.com

Aurinkolahden Peruskoulu
Leikosaarentie 17
Helsinki, 00980
Finland
Tel: +358 93 108 0857
Web site: www.auripk.edu.hel.fi

Australian Science and Mathematics School
Flinders University, Sturt Road
Bedford Park, SA, 5042
Australia
Tel: +61 8 8201 5686
Email: contactasms@sau.sa.gov.au
Web site: www.asms.sa.edu.au

Berufsschule für Gartenbau und Floristik
Donizettiweg 31
Vienna, 1220
Austria
Tel: +43 1 599 169 5860
Email: bs22doni031v@m56ssr.wien.at
Web site: www.wiener-berufsschulen.at/gf

Blásalir
Brekknaás 4
Reykjavik, 110
Iceland
Tel: +354 557 5720
Email: blasalir@leikskolar.rvk.is

Blyth Community College
Chase Farm Drive
Blyth, Northumberland, NE24 4JP
England, United Kingdom
Tel: +44 1670 798 100
Email: admin@bcc.uk.com
Web site: www.bcc.uk.com

Canning Vale College
26 Dumbarton Rd, Canning Vale

Perth, WA, 6155
Australia
Tel: +618 9334 9000
Email: tlc@cvc.wa.edu.au
Web site: www.cvc.wa.edu.au

Cégep de Sainte-Foy
2410, chemin Sainte-Foy
Sainte-Foy (Quebec), G1V 1T3
Canada
Tel: +1 418 659 6600
Email: mcmontminy@cegep-ste-foy.qc.ca
Web site: www.cegep-ste-foy.qc.ca

Centre de Formation des Nouvelles Technologies
75, rue Duquet
Sainte-Thérèse (Quebec), J7E 5R8
Canada
Tel: +1 450 433 5480
Email: infocfnt@cssmi.qc.ca
Web site: www.cfnt.qc.ca

Coláiste Eoin agus Coláiste Íosagáin
Bóthar Stigh Lorgan, Baile an Bhóthair
Co. Átha Cliath
Ireland
Tel: +353 1 288 4028
Email: Iosagain.ias@eircom.net

Collège « L'Esplanade »
Route de Saint-Cergue 5
Begnins, 1268
Switzerland
Tel: +41 22 366 4761
Email: eps.begnins@dfj.vd.ch

Collège Shawinigan
2263 avenue du Collège, C.P. 610
Shawinigan (Quebec), G9N 6V8
Canada
Tel: +1 819 539 6401
Email: ybellerive@collegeshawinigan.qc.ca
Web site: www.collegeshawinigan.qc.ca

The Community School of Auchterarder
New School Lane
Auchterarder, Perthshire, PH3 1BL
Scotland, United Kingdom
Tel: +44 176 466 2182
Email: headteacher@auchterarder.pkc.sch.uk
Web site: www.tcsoa.com

Cowgate Under 5's Centre
172 High Street, 7 Assembly Close

Edinburgh, EH1 1QX
Scotland, United Kingdom
Tel: +44 131 225 7251

Csapi Általános Iskola, Szakiskola, Diákotthon Kollégium
PetŒfi u. 7
Csapi, 8755
Hungary
Tel: +36 93 358 800
Email: kiefer@csapi.sulinet.hu

De Levensboom
Bruyningstraat 56 A
Kortrijk-Marke, 8510
Belgium
Tel: +32 5621 5154
Email: info@levensboom.be
Web site: www.levensboom.be

Ecole du Petit-Lancy
5, avenue du Louis-Bertrand
Petit-Lancy, Geneva, 1213
Switzerland
Tel: +41 22 792 2188

Escola E.B.I./J.I. da Malagueira
Av. Eng° Arantes Oliveira (Estrada das Piscinas)
Evora, 7000-758
Portugal
Tel: +35 26 675 0050

Fawood Children's Centre
35 Fawood Avenue, Stonebridge
London, NW10 8DX
England, United Kingdom
Tel: +44 208 965 9334
Email: sarah@fawoodcc.brent.sch.uk

Fjölbrautaskóli Snæfellinga
Grundargötu 44
Grundarfjörður, 350
Iceland
Tel: +354 430 8400
Email: gudbjorg@fsn.is
Web site: www.fsn.is

Fukushima Prefectural Koriyama School for the Physically Handicapped
1 Uenodai, Tomita-cho, Koriyama-shi
Fukushima, 963-8041
Japan
Tel: +81 024 951 0247
Email: school@koriyama-sh.fks.ed.jp
Web site: www.koriyama-sh.fks.ed.jp

Georgetown University Law Center
600 New Jersey Avenue, NW
Washington, DC, 20001
United States
Tel: +1 202 662 9054
Email: dmg47@law.georgetown.edu
Web site: www.law.georgetown.edu

Geumho Elementary School
511 Geumho 2ga-dong Seongdong-gu
Seoul, 133-803
Korea
Tel: +82 2 2238 3906
Web site: www.geumho.es.kr

**Griffeen Valley Educate
Together School**
Grffeen Glen Boulevard, Lucan
Co. Dublin
Ireland
Tel: +353 1 621 9819
Email: GriffeenValley@hotmail.com
Web site: www.gveducate.org

Groupe Scolaire Martin Peller
14, rue Passe Demoiselle
Reims, 51100
France
Tel: +33 3 2608 5193

**Gymnase du Bugnon – Site de
Sévelin**
Avenue de Sévélin 44
Lausanne, 1004
Switzerland
Tel: +41 21 557 8200
Email: gymnase.sevelin@edu-vd.ch
Web site: www.sevelin.dfj.vd.ch

**Gymnase et Centre
d'Enseignement
Professionnel de Morges**
Avenue de Marcelin 31, 33
Morges, 1110
Switzerland
Tel: +41 21 316 0420
Email: claude.felberbaum@dfj.vd.ch
Web site: www.gymnase-morges.ch

**Hampden Gurney Church of
England
Primary School**
Nutford Place
London, W1H5HA
England, United Kingdom
Tel: +44 207 641 4195

Harmony Primary School
Aurora Drive, Atwell
Perth, WA
Australia
Tel: +61 8 9498 6333

HEC Montréal
3000, chemin de la Côte-Sainte-Catherine
Montreal (Quebec), H3T 2A7
Canada
Tel: +1 514 340 6479
Web site: www.hec.ca

**Hosmarinpuisto School and Day
Care Centre**
Hösmärinahde 5
Espoo, 02760
Finland

**Ikeda Elementary School/
Osaka-Kyoiku University**
1-5-1 Midorigaoka, Ikeda-shi, Osaka
Osaka Pref., 583-0026
Japan
Tel: +81 72 761 3591
Email: ikeda-e@cc.osaka-kyoiku.ac.jp
Web site: www.ikeda-e.oku.ed.jp

Kaposvári Egyetem
Guba Sándor u. 40, Pf. 16
Kaposvár, 7400
Hungary
Tel: +36 82 314 155
Email: kszi@mail.atk.u-kaposvar.hu
Web site: www.u-kaposvar.hu

Kingsdale School
Alleyn Park, Dulwich
London, SE21 8SQ
England, United Kingdom
Tel: +44 208 675 7575
Email: info@kingsdale.southwark.sch.uk
Web site: www.kingsdale.southwark.sch.uk

Kingsmead Primary School
Off Dukes Way
Northwich, Cheshire, CW9 8WA
England, United Kingdom
Tel: +44 160 633 3470
Email: head@kingsmead.cheshire.gov.uk
Web site: www.kingsmead.cheshire.sch.uk

Laekjarskóli
Sólvangsvegur, 4
Hafnarfirdi, 220
Iceland
Tel: +354 555 0585

Email: skoli@laekjarskoli.is
Web site: www.laekjarskoli.is

Mawson Lakes School
Garden Terrace, Mawson Lakes
Adelaide, SA 5095
Australia
Tel: +61 8 8260 1681
Email: admin@mawsonlakes.sa.edu.au
Web site: www.mawsonlakes.sa.edu.au

Mindarie Senior College
Anchorage Drive, Mindarie
Perth, WA
Australia
Tel: +61 8 9304 5800
Email: info@mindarie.wa.edu.au
Web site: www.vianet.net.au/~wc1/msc

Mittelschule Carlbergergasse
Carlbergergasse 72
Vienna, 1230
Austria
Tel: +43 1 869 7623 211
Email: office@juniorhighschool.at
Web site: www.juniorhighschool.at

Morgan Academy
Forfar Road
Dundee, DD4 7AX
Scotland, United Kingdom
Tel: +44 1382 307 000
Email: morgan@dundeecity.gov.uk

Mossbourne Community Academy
100 Downs Park Road
Hackney, London, E5 8NP
England, United Kingdom
Tel: +44 208 525 5200
Email:
enquiries@mossbourne.hackney.sch.uk
Web site: www.mossbourne.hackney.sch.uk

National Maritime College
Ringaskiddy
Co. Cork
Ireland
Tel: +353 21 497 0600
Email: reception@nmci.ie
Web site: www.nmci.ie

**National University of Ireland,
Maynooth**
Kilcock Road, Maynooth
Co. Kildare
Ireland
Tel: +353 17 708 6023

Email: buildings.office@nuim.ie
Web site: www.nuim.ie

National University of Singapore High School of Mathematics and Science

20 Clementi Avenue 1
Singapore, 129957
Singapore
Tel: +65 6559 3283
Email: einstein@highsch.nus.edu.sg
Web site: www.highsch.nus.edu.sg

Nesting Primary School

Skellister, South Nesting
Shetland, ZE2 9PP
Scotland, United Kingdom
Tel: +44 159 574 3701
Email: nestinghead@shetland.biblio.net

Ngalilwara Study Centre (remote campus) for Batchelor Institute of Indigenous Tertiary Education

P.O. Box Batchelor
Batchelor, NT, 0845
Australia
Tel: +61 8 8946 3812
Email: glennis.bibra@batchelor.edu.au
Web site: www.batchelor.edu.au

North Kildare Educate Together School

Clane Road
Celbridge, Co. Kildare
Ireland
Tel: +353 1 627 4388
Email: nkets.ias@eircom.net
Web site: www.nkets.ie

Northlands-Nordelta

Av. De Los Colegios, 680
Nordelta, Buenos Aires, B1670NNN
Argentina
Tel: +54 11 4871 2668
Email: infonordel@northlands.org.ar
Web site: www.northlands.org.ar

Nuovo Complesso Scolastico di Monzambano

Comune di Monzambano, piazza Vittorio Emanuele 13
Monzambano, 46040
Italy
Tel: +39 03 7680 0502
Email: ufficiotecnico@comune.monzambano.mn.it
Web site: www.comune.monzambano.mn.it

Nyíregyházi Főiskola

Sóstói út 31/b
Nyíregyháza, 4400
Hungary
Tel: +36 42 599 400
Email: vads@nyf.hu
Web site: www.nyf.hu

Oteha Valley School

2 Medallion Drive, Albany
Aukland, 1311
New Zealand
Tel: +64 9 477 0033
Email: enquiries@oteha.school.nz
Web site: www.oteha.school.nz

Queen Anne High School

Broomhead Parks
Dunfermline, KY12 0PQ
Scotland, United Kingdom
Tel: +44 138 331 2620
Email: queenannehs.enquiries@fife.gov.uk
Web site: http://members.aol.com/qahs/

Rudolf Steinerschool – Leuven

Privaatweg 7
Wijgmaal (Leuven), 3018
Belgium
Tel: +32 16 202 954
Email: b.vanermen@tiscali.be

Seoul National School for the Blind

1-4 Shingyo-dong, Jongro-gu
Seoul, 110-032
Korea
Tel: +82 2 737 0652
Web site: www.bl.sc.kr

Shirokane Kindergarten

5-23-11 Shirokanedai Minato-ku
Tokyo, 108-0071
Japan
Tel: +81 33 441 8497
Web site: www8.ocn.ne.jp/~shiinoki

St. John Ambulance First Aid School

12304 – 118 Avenue
Edmonton (Alberta), T5L 5G8
Canada
Tel: +1 780 452 6161
Email: sjaedm@stjohn.ab.ca
Web site: www.stjohn.ab.ca

Szegedi Tudományegyetem Tanulmányi és Információs Központ

Szeged, 6722

Hungary
Tel: +36 62 546 600
Email: info@tik.u-szeged.hu
Web site: www.tik.u-szeged.hu

Tajimi Junior High School

4-10, Misaka-cho, Tajimi-shi
Gufu-ken, 507-0803
Japan
Tel: +81 3 0572 22 3327
Email: j-tajimi@city.tajimi.gufu.jp
Web site: www2.city.tajimi.gifu.jp

Te Matauranga School

Finlayson Avenue, Clendon, Manukau
Auckland
New Zealand
Tel: +64 9 266 9493
Email: office@tematauranga.school.nz

Türki Eğitim Derneği (TED) Ankara Koleji

Taflpinar Köyü Yumrubel Mevkii
Gölbafli, Ankara, 06830
Turkey
Tel: +90 312 586 9000
Email: info@tedankara.k12.tr
Web site: www.tedankara.k12.tr

Université du Québec à Montréal

C.P. 8888, Succ. Centre-ville
Montreal (Quebec), H3C 3P8
Canada
Tel: +1 514 987 3000
Email: buono.nicolas@uqam.ca
Web site: www.immobilier.uqam.ca

Unlimited Paenga Tawhiti

P.O. Box 4666, 263 High Street
Christchurch
New Zealand
Tel: +64 3 3777 773
Email: office@unlimited.school.nz
Web site: www.unlimited.school.nz

Viikini Normaalikoulu

Kevätkatu 2
Helsinki, 00780
Finland

Víkurskóli

Hamravík 10
Reykjavik, 112
Iceland
Tel: +354 545 2700
Email: vikurs@vikurskoli.is
Web site: www.vikurskoli.is

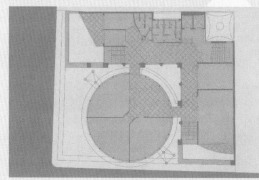

31st Primary School – Athens

The designs of the architectural study that was commissioned by the School Building Organization (SBO) of Greece concern the construction of the 31st Primary School of Athens for 180 students.

This study was made by the architect Stavros Vidalis for the pilot program "Open School" or "Community School" that SBO initiated in 2002 in view of constructing twenty new schools of this type. The general guidelines for the architectural construction, the design and the area tabulation form as well as the stated functions were determined by the civil engineer Manolis Baltas who was then the Chief Executive Manager of SBO. All of the above provided the widely-construed, political framework for the design of the Open Educational Space. These principles were approved by the Greek parliament which enacted a special law that furnished the institutional basis for the project of the Open School. The entire enterprise aims at making the school fully accessible after the end of the school day to the local society so that it might meet the current social needs.

According to the study of 31st Primary School by Stavros Vidalis, provision has been made for specific purpose spaces such as a music hall, dance hall, art and multimedia studios, theatre, amphitheatre, movie theatre and multi-purpose room, and four underground levels for parking. The architectural study aspired to combine the real with the imaginary, a sense of solid permanence with the gratifications of more ethereal forms, knowledge and utopia, education and playfulness.

Manolis Baltas is Vice-president and Managing Director of "REDEPLAN S.A. *Consultants"* a company which specialises in Project Management in the Greek and international market. As Educational Facilities Management Expert, Mr. Baltas has taken part in PEB/OECD expert committees addressing issues concerning the protection of buildings from the effects of earthquakes and the evaluation of the quality of the educational infrastructures. He has exclusive rights over intellectual property that is internationally recognized with the name ESBI-Qsystem (Evaluation School Building Indices Quality System). The ESBI-Qsystem aims to develop principles, methodology and reliable and effective criteria for evaluation of educational infrastructure.

The first step of the methodology is the implementation of a detailed survey of the existing infrastructure. The multi-purposes of the survey's results should be underlined: *The statistics and indicators of the ESBI-QSystem arise from a single school unit level and, gradually, accumulate in higher geographical and or administrative areas, thus the system can be applied in any area of different population size (community, municipality, prefecture, region, state).*

The ESBI-Qsystem can be a reliable tool for those responsible for planning and management of Educational Programs funded by International Institutes as the European Investment Bank (EIB), the council of Europe Development Bank (EDB), the World Bank (WB), the European Bank of Reconstruction and Development (EBRD), and similar institutions

The architect Stavros Vidalis is currently working in Greece. He has been conducting studies for public and private work projects and has participated in international architectural competitions.

For further information, contact:

Manolis Baltas
Civil Engineer
Educational Facilities
Management Expert
19 Marni St.
10433 Athens, Greece
Tel: 0030 2105229418
Fax: 0030 21 05220846
Email: info@baltas.gr

Stavros Vidalis
Architect
38 Xenodratous St.
10676 Athens, Greece
Tel: 0030 2107219830
Fax: 0030 2107222049
Email: vsaction2@yahoo.gr

Laekjarskóli
Á Stofunni – Arkitektar
Bergstadastraeti 10a
Reykjavik, 101
Iceland
Tel: +354 551 1460
Email: stofan@stofunni.is
Web site: www.stofunni.is

Nyíregyházi Föiskola
A Stúdio Kft
Dózsa Gy. u. 5
Nyíregyháza, 4400
Hungary
Tel: +36 42 500 112
Email: astudio@chello.hu

Te Matauranga School
ADA Ltd.
99 Great South Road,
Greenlane Auckland
New Zealand
Tel: +64 9 524 0437
Email: office@adamsdelamare.co.nz
Web site: www.adamsdelamare.co.nz

Queen Anne High School
AEDAS
Floor 9, No.1 Cadogan Square,
Cadogan Street
Glasgow, G2 7HF
Scotland, United Kingdom
Tel: +44 141 225 0555
Email: glasgow@aedas.com
Web site: www.aedas.com

Fawood Children's Centre
Alan Lai / Alsop Design Ltd.
Parkgate Studio
41 Parkgate Road
London, SW11 4NP
England, United Kingdom
Tel: +44 207 989 0383
Email: alai@alsoparchitects.com
Web site: www.alsoparchitects.com

Cowgate Under 5's Centre
Allan Murray Architects
9 Harrison Gardens
Edinburgh, EH11 1SJ
Scotland, United Kingdom

Tel: +44 131 313 1999
Email: AMA@AMA-ltd.co.uk
Web site: www.AMA-ltd.co.uk

The Community School of Auchterarder
Anderson Bell + Christie
382 Great Western Road
Glasgow, G4 9HT
Scotland, United Kingdom
Tel: +44 141 339 1515
Email: brucebrebner@andersonbellchristie.com
Web site: www.andersonbellchristie.com

Rudolf Steinerschool – Leuven
Architecten Bekker, Carnoy, Deru (ABCD)
Foneinstraat 1A bus 2
Leuven, 3000
Belgium
Tel: +32 16 207 200
Email: info@a33.be
Web site: www.a33.be

Viikin Normaalikoulu
Ark-house Arkkitehdit Oy
Pursimiehenkatu 26 C 53
Helsinki, 00150
Finland
Tel: +358 97 742 480
Email: markku.erholtz@ark-house.com

Berufsschule für Gartenbau und Floristik
Atelier 4 Architects
Windmühlgasse 26
Vienna, 1060
Austria
Tel: +43 1 587 2115
Email: office@at4-architects.at

Tajimi Junior High School
Atelier Zo
3-18-11, Matsubara, Setagaya-ku
Tokyo, 156-0043
Japan
Tel: +81 3 3324 0813
Email: atelierzo@zoz.co.jp
Web site: www.zoz.co.jp

Oteha Valley School
Babbage Consultants Ltd.
109 Fanshawe Street
Auckland
New Zealand
Tel: +64 9 379 9980
Email: admin@babbage.co.nz
Web site: www.babbage.co.nz

Csapi Általános Iskola, Szakiskola, Diákotthon Kollégium
Baratta Építész és Mérnök Iroda Kft.
Bíró Márton u. 71
Zalaegerszeg, 8900
Hungary
Tel: +36 92 348 247
Email: baratta-zambo@matavnet.hu

Nesting Primary School
Barbara Dinnage
Shetland Islands Council
Gremista, Lerwick
Shetland, ZE1 0PX
Scotland, United Kingdom
Tel: +44 159 574 4140
Email: Barbara.Dinnage@sic.shetland.gov.uk

Cégep de Sainte-Foy
Bélanger, Beauchemin Architectes
819, Av. Moreau
Sainte-Foy (Quebec), G1V 3B5
Canada
Tel: +1 418 653 8341
Email: info@groupea.qc.ca

Centre de Formation des Nouvelles Technologies
Bouré Therrien L'Ecuyer Lefaivre/ Hamelin Lalonde/ Birtz Bastien Architectes
7255, rue Alexandra, suite 201
Montreal (Quebec), H2R 2Y9
Canada
Tel: +1 514 273 4373
Email: info@bbbl.ca
Web site: www.bbaa.ca

Ngalilwara Study Centre
Build Up Design Architects Pty. Ltd.

P.O. Box 4128
Darwin, 0801
Australia
Tel: +61 8 89 816 646
Email: s.scally@octa4.net.au

**Hampden Gurney Church
of England Primary School**
Building Design Partnership
16 Brewhouse Yard
Clerkenwell, London, EC1V 4LJ
England, United Kingdom
Tel: +44 207 812 8000
Email: enquiries@bdp.co.uk
Web site: www.bdp.co.uk

National Maritime College
Building Design Partnership
Blackhall Green
Dublin, 7
Ireland
Tel: +353 1 474 0600
Email: Dublin@bdp.ie
Web site: www.bdp.ie

Gymnase du Bugnon – Site de Sévelin
CCHE Architecture SA
Av. Tivoli 2, C.P. 5623
Lausanne, 1002
Switzerland
Tel: +41 21 321 44 66
Email: admin@cche-architecture.ch
Web site: www.cche-architecture.ch

École du Petit-Lancy
**CLR Chevalley Longchamp
Russbach Architectes fas sia**
8, rue des Vieux-Grenadiers
Geneva, 1205
Switzerland
Tel: +41 22 322 2900
Email: info@clr.ch
Web site: www.clr.ch

**Griffeen Valley Educate
Together School
National University
of Ireland, Maynooth**
Coady Partnership Architects
Trinity House, Charleston Road, Ranelagh

Dublin, 6
Ireland
Tel: +353 1 497 6766
Email: admin@coady.ie
Web site: www.coady.ie

**Gymnase et Centre d'Enseignement
Professionnel de Morges**
Consortium Planification Marcelin
GeninascaDelefortrie SA et
Tekhne Management SA
Rue de la Place-d'Armes 3
Neuchâtel, 2001
Switzerland
Tel: +41 32 729 9960
Email: gd@gd-archi.ch
Web site: www.gd-archi.ch

**National University of Singapore High
School of Mathematics and Science**
CPG Consultants Pte. Ltd.
238B Thomson Road #18-00 Tower B
Novena Square
Singapore, 307685
Singapore
Tel: +65 6357 4468
Email: phan.pit.li@cpgcorp.com.sg
Web site: www.cpgcorp.com.sg

Kingsmead Primary School
**Craig White, White Design
Associates Ltd.**
The Proving House,
101 Sevier Street Bristol, BS2 9LB
England, United Kingdom
Tel: +44 117 954 7333
Email: info@white-design.co.uk
Web site: www.white-design.co.uk

HEC Montréal
**Dan S. Hanganu et
Jodoin, Lamarre, Pratte et
Associés**
404, rue Saint-Dizier
Montreal (Quebec), H2Y 3T3
Canada
Tel: +1 514 288 1890
Email: dhanganu@hanganu.com

Kaposvári Egyetem
Dezsö Töreky
Törökvész út 88/a.
Budapest, 1025
Hungary
Tel: +36 1 326 1880
Email: tus@t-online.hu
Web site: www.tus.hu

Groupe Scolaire Martin Peller
**Dominique Coulon – Cabinet
Coulon**
5, Quai de Paris
Strasbourg, 67000
France
Tel: +33 3 8832 1761
Email: agence@coulon-architectes.fr

Mindarie Senior College
Donaldson + Warn, Architects
38 Roe Street
Perth, WA, 6000
Australia
Tel: +61 8 9328 4475
Email: admin@donaldsonandwarn.com.au
Web site: www.donaldsonandwarn.com.au

Seoul National School for the Blind
Dowoo Architects Associates Ltd.
149-18, Samsung-Dong, Kangnam-Gu
Seoul, 135-090
Korea
Tel: +82 2 511 1300
Email: dowoo@dowoo.com
Web site: www.dowoo.com

Kingsdale School
dRMM Architects
no. one Centaur Street
London, SE1 7EG
England, United Kingdom
Tel: +44 207 803 0777
Email: alex@drmm.co.uk
Web site: www.drmm.co.uk

Morgan Academy
**Dundee City Council, Architectural
Services**
Floors 11/12 Tayside House,
28 Crichton Street
Dundee, DD1 3RQ

Scotland, United Kingdom
Tel: +44 1382 433 640
Email: john.porter@dundeecity.gov.uk

Geumho Elementary School
Garam Architects & Associates
563-17, Shinsa-Dong, Kangnam-Gu
Seoul, 135-891
Korea
Tel: +82 2 511 0361
Email: garam563@chol.com

Ardscoil Mhuire
Coláiste Eoin agus Coláiste Íosagáin
North Kildare Educate Together
School
Grafton Architects
12 Dame Court
Dublin, 2
Ireland
Tel: +353 1 671 3365
Email: info@graftonarchitects.ie
Web site: www.graftonarchitects.ie

Canning Vale College
HASSELL
Podium Level, Central Park
152-158 St. Georges Tce
Perth, 6000
Australia
Tel: +618 9288 8500
Email: perth@hassell.com.au
Web site: www.hassell.com.au

De Levensboom
Isabelle Jacques and Bernard
Wittevrongel
President Rooseveltplein 5
Kortrijk, 8500
Belgium
Tel: +32 5620 0438
Email: jacquesisabelle@skynet.be

Escola E.B.I./J.I. da Malagueira
J. Farelo Pinto-Gabinete de
Arquitectura, Lda.
Rua 4 da Infantaria, 40, r/c dto.
Lisbon, 1350-273
Portugal
Tel: +35 21 387 5945
Email: farelopinto@mail.telepac.pt

Northlands-Nordelta
Jeffrey Berk and Fernando Diez
Tucuman 2762
Olivos, B 1636 DCJ
Argentina
Tel: +54 11 4799 2950
Email: jeffberk@uolsinectis.com.ar

Aurinkolahden Peruskoulu
Jeskanen-Repo-Teränne
Arkkitehdit Oy &
Arkkitehtitoimisto Leena
Yli-Lonttinen Ky
Pursimiehenkatu 29-31 B 519
Helsinki, 00150
Finland
Tel: +358 96 844 4815
Email: tuomo.repo@jrt-ark.com
Web site: www.jrt-ark.com

Mittelschule Carlbergergasse
Johannes Zieser, ziesar Architekt
Marc Aurel-Straße 3
Vienna, 1010
Austria
Tel: +43(1)5332386-0
Email: office@zieserarchitekt.com
Web site: www.zieserarchitekt.com

Fukushima Prefectural Koriyama
School for the Physically
Handicapped
Kazuo Watabe / Yui Architects &
Planners
Kagurazaka FN Bldg., 8F
6 – 6, 7 – 1 Kagurazaka, shinjyuku-ku
Tokyo, 162-0825
Japan
Tel: +81 033 267 5512
Email: yui-kenchiku@nifty.com
Web site: www.yui-kenchiku.com

Ikeda Elementary School/
Osaka-Kyoiku University
Kyodo Sekkei
5-10-14 Nishi-Tenman, Kita-ku, Osaka-shi
Osaka Pref., 530-0047
Japan
Tel: +81 6 6364 5836

Email: Osaka@kyodo-sekkei.com
Web site: www.kyodo-sekkei.com

Collège Shawinigan
Les Architectes Michel Pellerin,
Sylvie Rainville, Renée Tremblay
569, 5e Rue
Shawinigan (Quebec), G9N 1E7
Canada
Tel: +1 819 536 0388
Email: renee.tremblay@gestact.com

St. John Ambulance First Aid School
Manasc Isaac Architects Ltd.
10225 – 100 Avenue
Edmonton (Alberta), T5J 0A1
Canada
Tel: +1 780 429 3977
Email: vivian@miarch.com
Web site: www.miarch.com

Blásalir
Manfred Vilhjalmsson and Steinar
Sigurdsson
Skolavordustigur 12
Reykjavik, 101
Iceland
Tel: +354 530 6990

Mawson Lakes School
MGT Canberra Architects (now
Guida Moseley Brown Architects)
and Russell & Yelland Architects
PO Box 3054
101 Frederick Street
Unley, SA, 5063
Australia
Tel: +61 88 271 4555
Email: jfheld@rusyel.com.au
Web site: www.gmbarchitects.com
www.rusyel.com.au

Shirokane Kindergarten
Mitsuhiro Suda
9-1-7-903 Akasaka Minato-ku
Tokyo, 107-0052
Japan
Tel: +81 33 401 8898
Email: ssudda@syd.odn.ne.jp

Collège « L'Esplanade »
Pascal de Benoit & Martin Wagner Architectes SA
Ch. Entre-Bois 2bis
Lausanne, 1018
Switzerland
Tel: +41 21 647 3080
Email: debenoit-wagner@bluewin.ch
Web site: www.debenoit-wagner.ch

Nuovo Complesso
Scolastico di Monzambano
Politecnico di Milano – Dipartimento BEST
Via Ponzio 31
Milano, 20133
Italy
Tel: +39 02 2399 6007
Email: ettore.zambelli@polimi.it
Web site: www.polimi.it

Mossbourne Community Academy
Richard Rogers Partnership
Thames Wharf Studios, Rainville Road
London, W6 9HA
England, United Kingdom
Tel: +44 207 385 1235
Email: enquiries@rrp.co.uk
Web site: www.rrp.co.uk

Türk Egitim Dernegi (TED)
Ankara Koleji
Semra Uygur, Özcan Uygur - Uygur Mimarlik Ltd.
Büklüm Sok. No. 68/2 Kavaklidere
Ankara, 06700
Turkey
Tel: +90 312 467 6090
Email: semra@uygurmimarlik.com.tr

Georgetown University Law Center
Shepley Bullfinch Richardson and Abbott
40 Broad Street
Boston, MA, 02109
United States
Tel: +1 617 423 1700
Email: jroper@sbra.com
Web site: www.sbra.com

Víkurskóli
Sigurdur Gústafsson
Túngötu 5
Reykjavik, 101
Iceland
Tel: +354 568 5097

Szegedi Tudományegyetem
Tanulmányi es Információs
Központ
Szántó & Mikó Épitészek Kft.
Budapest, 1052
Hungary
Tel: +36 12 667 870
Email: szm@axelero.hu
Web site: www.szantoesmiko.hu

Harmony Primary School
Taylor Robinson Architects
234 Railway Parade
West Leederville, WA 6007
Australia
Tel: +61 8 9388 6111
Email: admin@tayrob.com.au
Web site: www.tayrob.com.au

Université du Québec à Montréal
Tétreault Parent Languedoc et Associés/Saia Barbarese Architectes
401, rue Notre-Dame Est
Montreal (Quebec), H2Y 1C9
Canada
Tel: +1514 848 0808
Email: mlanguedoc@aedifica.com
Web site: www.aedifica.com

Fjölbrautaskóli Snæfellinga
VA Arkitektar, Indro Candi and Sigurꝺur Björgúlfsson
Skolavordustigur 12
Reykjavik, 101
Iceland
Tel: +354 530 6990
Email: indro@vaarkitektar.is
Web site: www.vaarkitektar.is

Blyth Community Collage
Waring & Netts
Arcadia House, Balliol Business Park,
Benton Lane
Newcastle Upon Tyne, NE12 8EW
England, United Kingdom
Tel: +44 191 266 6900
Email: newcastle@waring.co.uk
Web site: www.waring-netts.co.uk

Arabian Peruskoulu
Wartiainen Architects (Evata Finland)
P.O. Box 393
Helsinki, 00100
Finland
Tel: +358 9 4130 300
Email: vesa.peltonen@evata.com
Web site: www.evata.com

Australian Science and
Mathematics School
Woods Bagot
GPO Box 338
Adelaide, SA, 5001
Australia
Tel: +61 8 8212 7600
Email: andrew.ford@woodsbagot.com.au

Unlimited Paenga Tawhiti
Wynyard Design Ltd.
Unit 12, 10 Acheron Drive, P.O. Box 80021
Christchurch
New Zealand
Tel: +64 3 341 8885
Email: wynyard.design@xtra.co.nz
Web site: www.wynyarddesign.co.nz

Hosmarinpuisto School and Day
Care Centre
Yrjö Suonto
Oravannahkatori 1
Espoo, 02120
Finland
Tel: +35 89 452 0520
Email: studio.suonto@pingrid.fi

Chapter 1 | Special Mentions

- **Fawood Children's Centre** – United Kingdom (England) – New building   ◆ ■ ▲ ▼
- **Hampden Gurney Church of England Primary** – United Kingdom (England) – New building   ◆   ▼ ★
- **Hosmarinpuisto School and Day Care Centre** – Finland – New building   ◆ ■ ▲
- **Rudolf Steiner School - Leuven** – Belgium – New building   ◆ ■ ▲ ▼ ★
- **Víkurskóli** – Iceland – New building   ◆ ■ ▲
- **Fukushima Pref. Koriyama Sch./Handicapped** – Japan – New building   ◆   ▼
- **Canning Vale College** – Australia – Extension   ◆ ■ ▲
- **Kingsdale School** – United Kingdom (England) – Extension   ◆ ■
- **HEC Montréal** – Canada – Renovation   ◆ ■ ▲

Chapter 2 | Multiple Levels

- **The Community School of Auchterarder** – United Kingdom (Scotland) – New building   ◆ ■ ▼
- **Türk Eğitim Derneği (TED) Ankara Koleji** – Turkey – New building   ◆ ■
- **Mittelschule Carlbergergasse** – Austria – New building   ◆ ■ ★
- **Seoul National School for the Blind** – Korea – New building   ■ ▼
- **Arabian Peruskoulu** – Finland – Renovation   ◆ ■ ▲
- **Aurinkolahden Peruskoulu** – Finland – New building   ◆ ■ ★
- **Collège « L'Esplanade »** – Switzerland – Extension   ◆ ▼
- **Escola E. B. I./J. I. da Malagueira, Évora** – Portugal – New building   ◆ ■
- **Lækjarskóli** – Iceland – New building   ◆ ■ ▲
- **Northlands-Nordelta** – Argentina – New building   ◆ ■
- **Nuovo Complesso Scolastico di Monzambano** – Italy – New building   ◆ ■ ▲
- **Csapi Általános Iskola, Szakiskola, D. Koll.** – Hungary – Extension and renovation   ■ ▲
- **Viikin Normaalikoulu** – Finland – New building   ◆ ■
- **NUS High School of Mathmatics and Science** – Singapore – New building   ◆ ▲
- **Gymnase et Centre d'Ens. Prof. de Morges** – Switzerland – New building   ▲

Chapter 3 | Pre-primary and Primary Level

- **Blásalir** – Iceland – New building   ◆ ▼
- **Cowgate Under 5's Centre** – United Kingdom (Scotland) – New building   ◆ ■ ▼
- **Shirokane Kindergarten** – Japan – New building   ◆ ■
- **Groupe Scolaire Martin Peller** – France – New building   ◆ ■
- **Harmony Primary School** – Australia – New building   ◆ ■ ▲
- **De Levensboom** – Belgium – New building   ◆ ■
- **École du Petit-Lancy** – Switzerland – New building   ◆
- **Geumho Elementary School** – Korea – New building   ◆ ■ ★